MYSTERY VOICES

MORE WILDSIDE CLASSICS

Dacobra, or The White Priests of Ahriman, by Harris Burland
The Nabob, by Alphonse Daudet
Out of the Wreck, by Captain A. E. Dingle
The Elm-Tree on the Mall, by Anatole France
The Lance of Kanana, by Harry W. French
Amazon Nights, by Arthur O. Friel
Caught in the Net, by Emile Gaboriau
The Gentle Grafter, by O. Henry
Raffles, by E. W. Hornung
Gates of Empire, by Robert E. Howard
Tom Brown's School Days, by Thomas Hughes
The Opium Ship, by H. Bedford Jones
The Miracles of Antichrist, by Selma Lagerlof
Arsène Lupin, by Maurice LeBlanc
A Phantom Lover, by Vernon Lee
The Iron Heel, by Jack London
The Witness for the Defence, by A.E.W. Mason
The Spider Strain and Other Tales, by Johnston McCulley
Tales of Thubway Tham, by Johnston McCulley
The Prince of Graustark, by George McCutcheon
Bull-Dog Drummond, by Cyril McNeile
The Moon Pool, by A. Merritt
The Red House Mystery, by A. A. Milne
Blix, by Frank Norris
Wings over Tomorrow, by Philip Francis Nowlan
The Devil's Paw, by E. Phillips Oppenheim
Satan's Daughter and Other Tales, by E. Hoffmann Price
The Insidious Dr. Fu Manchu, by Sax Rohmer
Mauprat, by George Sand
The Slayer and Other Tales, by H. de Vere Stacpoole
Penrod (Gordon Grant Illustrated Edition), by Booth Tarkington
The Gilded Age, by Mark Twain
The Blockade Runners, by Jules Verne
The Gadfly, by E.L. Voynich

Please see www.wildsidepress.com for a complete list!

MYSTERY VOICES

*Interviews
with British Crime Writers*

**Conducted by
DALE SALWAK**

Citrus College

WILDSIDE PRESS

Copyright © 1991 by Dale Salwak

All rights reserved. No part of this book my be reproduced in any form without the expressed written consent of the publisher.

MYSTERY VOICES

This edition published in 2006 by Wildside Press, LLC.
www.wildsidepress.com

CONTENTS

Introduction: "On Being a Writer of Detective Fiction," by Catherine Aird		5
1.	Catherine Aird	11
2.	P. D. James	35
3.	H. R. F. Keating	58
4.	Ruth Rendell	81
5.	Julian Symons	95
About Dale Salwak		108
Index		109

ILLUSTRATIONS

P. D. James and Dale Salwak	4
Catherine Aird	14
P. D. James	38
H. R. F. Keating	58
Ruth Rendell	84
Julian Symons	98

For Eddie and Amy Dawes

P. D. James and Dale Salwak

INTRODUCTION

ON BEING A WRITER OF DETECTIVE FICTION

by Catherine Aird

It is not an accident that I have chosen an elegant and old-fashioned title to use as an introduction to the five interviews with writers of detective fiction which follow. In some quarters the construction of such stories is thought to be a curiously old-fashioned occupation, redolent of that Golden Age of the detective novel placed so firmly by the literary historians between the wars, and somewhat set apart from the fast-moving, action-packed thriller and the labyrinthine espionage novel.

My title, though, is I hope a little reminiscent of the eighteenth century, too. Addison and Steele might have taken it for an essay subject in *The Spectator* of the time, had the writing of detective fiction been a feature of their day. It wasn't, of course, because although they had the crime they didn't have the fiction.

In an earlier age still Francis Bacon, who was never prolix, would probably have had a simpler title. Perhaps "On Crime," or more penetratingly, "On Evil." But in his day the average citizen—let alone the average reader—did not have to turn to the reading of fiction for his excitement. Life itself in Tudor England had its own built-in hazards and there was nothing in the least vicarious about them, either. The dangers were for real, so to speak, and known and feared by all. The sentiment expressed in the popular saying, "Far from Court, far from danger," wasn't just an aphorism for Elizabethan courtiers.

The risks of—and to—life in the second half of the twentieth century are probably no less than those in earlier times, but—the motor vehicle excepted—they are less immediately obvious. Smoking and over-eating and lack of physical exercise (are health educators by way of being today's Puritans, I wonder?) have a lack of drama about them as life-threateners. Far more interesting is to read of stirring events in

Inspector Ghote's India, in the catchment area of the East Anglian Forensic Laboratory consulted by Adam Dalgliesh, and the not-so-gentle English villages in the imaginary county of Calleshire; to say nothing of the chilly worlds delineated by Ruth Rendell.

The authors of these countries of make-believe enjoy a freedom of action limited only by what is probable. Mark that I did not write "possible." That truth is stranger than fiction is universally allowed. Its converse is seldom stated—that fiction is not allowed to be as strange as truth. As the French writer Corneille said, "The unlikely which did happen is less good for the story than the likely which didn't." (He also wrote, "Conquest without danger is a barren triumph," a fact appreciated by authors as well as generals.)

The ironic corollary to truth being stranger than fiction is that writing about the improbable therefore remains the preserve of the biographer and the chronicler of straight history. Jane Austen, who is the heroine of at least two of the five interviewees hereinafter subscribed (so to say), would no doubt have been able to summon up a pithy comment on that. I am not sure, though, where she would have placed the writers of science fiction and satire in a league table of truth versus fiction in *Brave New World* or *1984*. (Those who wonder what manner of detective story England's Jane would have written are referred to the way in which the clues about the piano are so expertly strewed about in "Emma.")

Probability is not a great constraint. Seen in this light, the hoary phrase "the bounds of probability" is not a *cliché* at all, but rather the definition of the size of canvas on which the detective novelist works. I think that reading these interviews will leave the reader with the awareness that we all feel when we have ample space in which to write. Julian Symons goes even further, observing that reality is almost always clumsy and inartistic.

Another feature which becomes apparent too is that we all share a freedom of choice in what we are writing about. P. D. James makes the point when she says every writer is trying to satisfy himself and his own talent, and H. R. F. Keating underlines another facet of that freedom when he says that he does not feel that anybody has had an influence on his writing.

What is so interesting is that the scope of the detective story is so broad that we are all able to find that freedom in such different locales, with completely different hero-figures, and with the spotlight of our individual interest and expertise focused on widely varying aspects of contemporary life. What we would seem to have in common is the enjoyment with which we travel in these worlds of our own creation.

And why not? Saving only that some things—undetectable poisons, for instance—are not considered quite fair, we are, in at least one sense (the modest one), masters of creation. We are able to change fictional circumstances with the stroke of a pen. There is no reason, therefore, why we should not have things exactly as we want them. That *pons asinorum* of early chemistry and physics lessons, the statement that all matter is indestructible and cannot be created, has no place in our work.

Something else which emerges from a study of these interviews is how valuable we have all subsequently found our early experiences at home and work to be. While in no sense writing autobiographically (and sometimes very consciously not doing so), that which we have learned and noticed inevitably finds its way—however transmogrified—into our writing. P. D. James's years as a senior administrator in the forensic and criminal departments of the Home Office have obviously come into their own, and H. R. F. Keating's early childhood as the son of a preparatory school headmaster have been put to good effect too. In the course of a misspent youth I was myself (for nine years) the chairman of a Burial Committee which administered a cemetery, an invaluable grounding (if you will forgive the pun) for any crime writer. With Ruth Rendell it was the unhappiness of her parents that had a formative effect.

The diversity of these backgrounds and experience is oddly unimportant. As you will see as you read, what matters is what is brought from them to the writing that is done. Something else which is surprisingly irrelevant is whether the writer is taking the miniscule view of the miniaturist, or the all-encompassing stance of the landscape painter on the broad canvas. It is said of two of England's most famous universities that at one an undergraduate learns everything about nothing and at the other nothing about everything. I think that the non-specialization of the latter is more to my own inclination, although I must confess to having learned a great deal about India from reading about Inspector Ghote, and about forensic pathology from a study of the works of P. D. James. (Would it be proper to call these *a corpus*?)

Comparisons are odorous, as Dogberry so wisely said (now there's a fictional policeman for you), but reading these interviews will disclose that another of the things we have in common is an ability to find satisfaction in writing about crime *per se*. There may be food for thought—and perhaps a thesis—there. Morbidity and mortality, murder and mayhem, are not everybody's choice of subject.

Another point for further study is something that only Ruth Rendell has chosen to talk about: the effect that being crime writers has had on our subsequent lives and ways of thought. I find this an interesting aspect of writing within the genre. The memory of a close examination of a long list of medical murderers which I did for literary purposes always rears its ugly head as I step into a doctor's consulting room. Loose talk about happy families inevitably prompts the recall of gruesome statistics about real-life murderers—if that isn't a contradiction in terms. (The statistician who was drowned in a river whose average depth was six inches is a story dear to my heart.) According to the figures most murders are family affairs and nearly all male murderers are widowers—not nice things to remember in domestic circles.

In fact my own experience is that all is grist to the mystery mill and that memory becomes geared to the recall of scenes useful to the page—and to the subject in hand. Observation of that "fair field, full of folk" which is humanity, becomes dangerously slanted towards crime. Even innocent phrases take on a sinister connotation. Perhaps one day a diligent bibliographer will do a study of the titles of detective stories—they would reap a rich harvest of *double entendre*. There's a converse there, too. I fear an off-duty crime writer (if such there be) would have as his or her first reaction to reading Thomas Gray's "Ode on the Death of a Favourite Cat" the unworthy thought "did it fall or was it pushed?"

I do not think, though, that I can go as far as saying that the crime writer has a unique psychology: only that some characteristics come in very handy. The insatiable curiosity of the elephant's child is something that I am sure no crime writer would wish to be without. A keen sense of observation I would rate as very important—that high degree of observation that not only notices the fact, but also goes on to ask why things should be as they are.

Something that is probably peculiar to crime writers is the linking of this curiosity and observation to the morbid side of human nature. Or are they just at one end of the scale of all writing which deals with the eternal conflict between good and evil? Julian Symons's view of the crime story as serious literature could not, I feel, have been better put; it would be interesting to have it even further explored. A feature that crime writers share with writers of other genres is an interest in exploring the outcome of the juxtaposition of circumstances. Dignified in the straight novel as a sub-plot, in the detective field this is engagingly known as a red herring.

Notwithstanding what I have written about specialization, a knowledge of the truly recondite is very useful to the crime writer. In my youth I learned a great deal about trains and railways from the works of Freeman Wills Crofts, and can never hear church bells on Sundays without being reminded of D. L. Sayers's book, *The Nine Tailors*. I share with P. D. James a great admiration of Dorothy L. Sayers's writing, finding that I still discover fresh nuggets of delight at each re-reading: the true test of greatness.

Another great benefit to the crime writer is an interest in the collection of unconsidered trifles of information. The detective story is not nearly so narrow a discipline as some would have the reader believe. There are very few aspects of life that cannot be accommodated within its compass, and there is no excuse for inattention to life's curiosities.

The ears, too, have their duties as well as the eyes. A capacity to listen almost indefinitely to people talking is a facility shared, I am sure, by all crime writers. A chance conversation overheard, or a casual exchange in the course of normal life, can be as rewarding as a day's conscientious study and research.

This raises the interesting question of the role of the author *quae* participant: the involvement referred to by P. D. James. I do not see how the reader is going to be involved if the writer isn't—although I can also appreciate the view advanced elsewhere of the writer as a camera.

Lest, though, I place the writing of detective fiction too high up the literary ladder, I will put on record a grass roots and very revealing experience I had far removed from the groves of Academe. A friend in a neighboring small village was suddenly consigned to hospital. It was a village without a library building. Books are supplied twice a week from a few shelves at the back of the village hall and the entire stock changed by the County Library every three months. It was this friend's duty to be present when the library supplies van called to take away the old stock and bring in new books. She was responsible for selecting those she thought her readers would like for the next three months.

After expressing a willingness to undertake this task on her behalf, I had a happy couple of days making up a balanced list of what every village should have in the way of history, biography, fiction (pure, detective and science), comedy, satire—(question: What is the difference between comedy and satire? Answer: In most countries, prison)—verse, reference books, and so forth.

Standing by her hospital bed I got very different marching orders. "Pick up the entire stock of westerns first," she said, "and then all the romance and science fiction you can lay your hands on. If you've still got room after that you could use up the rest of your allowance on mysteries. Some people quite like them."

I do hope that these interviews give pleasure to those who enjoy reading about both authors and the art and craft of writing detective fiction. Nowhere perhaps are art and craft so happily married as in the genre of the mystery novel. It is a sobering reflection that the only word that is at one and the same time a synonym of both the words "art" and "craft" is guile.

Think on that....

A CATHERINE AIRD CHRONOLOGY

1930 Kinn Hamilton McIntosh born June 20th at Huddersfield, Yorkshire, England.

1934 Attended Wentworth School.

1935 Attended Waverley School.

1941 Attended Greenhead High School (through 1946).

1966 The author's first novel, *The Religious Body*, is published under the pseudonym Catherine Aird by Macdonald & Co. in England, and by Doubleday & Co. in the United States (her joint publishers through 1969).

1967 *A Most Contagious Game*, Aird's second mystery novel, is selected by critic Anthony Boucher as one of thirteen outstanding crime novels of 1967.

1968 *Henrietta Who?*

1969 *The Complete Steel.*

1970 *The Complete Steel* is published in the U.S. under the title *The Stately Home Murder*. *A Late Phoenix* appears in England from Collins (her new British publisher); the American edition appears in 1971.

1972 Aird edits *Sturry: The Changing Scene* (nonfiction).

1973 Publication of *His Burial Too*. *The Story of Sturry*, a play, is produced in England.

1974 One of the author's few short stories, "The Scales of Justice," is published in *Argosy* (London edition, February).

1975 Aird edits another local history publication, *Fordwich: The Lost Port*. *Slight Mourning*, Aird's seventh mystery novel, is published by Collins (U.S. edition, 1976). Begins serving as Chairman of the Finance Committee, Girl Guides Association, London (the British equivalent of the Girl Scouts).

1977 *Parting Breath* appears from Collins (U.S. edition, 1978).

1979 *Some Die Eloquent* is published in England (U.S. edition, 1980). Aird edits *Chislet and Westbere, Villages of the Stour Lathe*.

1980 *Passing Strange*, the author's tenth mystery, is published by Collins (Doubleday edition, 1981).

1982 Publishes *Last Respects* and *The Six Preachers of Canterbury Cathedral* (edited volume).

1984 *Harm's Way*.

1985 Awarded Honorary Master's Degree, Kent University, Canterbury. Serves as Chairman of the Crime Writers Association Non-Fiction Awards Panel (through 1989).

1986 *A Dead Liberty*.

1988 Awarded MBE by the British Government.

1990 Publishes *The Body Politic* (U.S. edition, 1991). Serves as Chairman of the Crime Writers Association Fiction Awards Committee (through 1991).

Catherine Aird

I.
AN INTERVIEW WITH CATHERINE AIRD

SALWAK: "Catherine Aird" is a pseudonym; why don't you use your real name on your books?

AIRD: My Christian name is a very unusual one of Kinn. It is derived from my mother's maiden surname of Kinnis. My surname is McIntosh. When my first book was accepted I was told to go away and get myself a name that people would recognize as a man or a woman. I was told secondly that nobody in the U.S. would know how to pronounce any word beginning with "McI." I don't think this is true for a moment, but I came home and went through the family tree and worked my way backwards until I came to a great-great-grandmother called Catherine Aird, and decided that that would have to be my choice.

SALWAK: She was a writer?

AIRD: Actually, I think she was a midwife.

SALWAK: Were there *any* other writers in your family?

AIRD: Not to my knowledge, no.

SALWAK: Did your family support your choice of a career?

AIRD: Well, my father was a critic first and foremost, and very exacting to himself and to other people. He would always look for faults first. If he could find something wrong in any situation he always did. I think he was probably a practising pessimist of a rather high order. He would read everything, and was always inclined to look for things to criticize. But in a way living with this kind of attitude probably does jack your own sense up a bit; if you know that somebody is going to find fault with everything you do, then you try to make sure there aren't any faults to be found.

SALWAK: What about your mother?

AIRD: She really didn't approve of detective fiction, and kept telling me I ought to be writing something other than murder stories. But it's now become rather a way of life for me. One thing very interesting about this situation: during her liftime she was able to take one of my books when I'd just written the first couple of chapters, go away and write down the name of the murderer, put it into an envelope, and not open it until the end of the book. She could *always* identify the murderer, which had to have been a purely intuitive process. I must have subconsciously given away the killer in a way that I didn't think I could. I think this was because she knew me as a person.

SALWAK: Why crime fiction?

AIRD: I was a voracious reader of crime stories before I took to writing them, and I suppose that this is what led me to a life of crime. I went from reader to a writer. I don't know whether that's exactly gamekeeper-turned-poacher or poacher-turned-gamekeeper.

Also, I very much enjoy the writing of detective fiction: it has never seemed like work to me. I was once waiting for a friend who was a newspaper editor. I was going to meet him and his wife at the station, and their train was late. His wife got very agitated to think that I was standing at the station waiting for them, and he said something to her that I thought very true, because he too was a writer. He said, "Oh, no, she's a writer. Writers are never bored wherever they are."

I have thought about this quite a lot, and I think it is really substantially very true. It doesn't really matter where you're standing—even at a railway station doing nothing. If you're a writer you're still working. It means everything you do, and every situation you find yourself in, is potential grist to the mill. When I first began writing I was too self-conscious to whip out a pen and paper and write down a piece of dialogue or something. Now, several decades later, I'm less self-conscious, and I'll now make notes rather than rush around trying to remember everything I'm supposed to include.

SALWAK: Are there any occupational hazards in being a detective writer?

AIRD: People are very kind. They'll come right up to you at any time and tell you very good ways of committing a murder.

SALWAK: And do you use these tidbits?

AIRD: Not that I'm aware of!

SALWAK: What writers have influenced you?

AIRD: I have always been a great admirer of Dorothy L. Sayers. I have also enjoyed Margery Allingham and Josephine Tey. When I was a bit younger, it was people like John Buchan, Sapper, and Dorothy Yates—I devoured everything of theirs that I could lay my hands on. As I grew up I moved on to detective fiction.

SALWAK: Just what interested you about these writers?

AIRD: I just enjoyed them as a genre. I can remember some very early locked-door mysteries made quite an impression on me, books by John Dickson Carr, *The Chinese Orange Mystery* by Ellery Queen, and "The Speckled Band" by Conan Doyle, for example. I always found them an interesting puzzle.

SALWAK: Why should a younger writer want to read the likes of Sayers, Tey, or Allingham?

AIRD: Because they're so good; that's the only reason. They all wrote extremely well. I read them for pure admiration and enjoyment.

SALWAK: And whom do you read now?

AIRD: I am a devoted admirer of Emma Lathen, whom I think is your greatest American detective writer. I also enjoy a great deal of history and biography. I don't read much straight fiction now, but I do try to get through as many detective stories as I can, I think mostly from a great fear that one may be using the same sort of theme as somebody else. There's no point in reworking a theme if another writer has just brought out a book on the same subject. One has to be quite careful about this.

SALWAK: What about mainstream novelists?

AIRD: I admire Jane Austen very much. I wish I had her irony. I'm a great admirer of irony.

SALWAK: Would you agree that the 1930s and 1940s represent a golden age in detective fiction, that the 1950s and 1960s were a dry spell, and that we are now seeing a rejuvenation of the genre?

AIRD: Well, I don't know how much of a dry spell there really was. I first began reading detective fiction seriously during what you call the dry spell, and I wasn't aware of it being dry at all. There were still a great many people writing, not all of them household names, but men and women who were writing very well indeed, and whom I enjoyed reading very much, including Josephine Tey, Harry Carmichael, and Patricia Wentworth.

SALWAK: Do these cycles portend any changes in the future direction of the genre?

AIRD: I think the great thing about crime fiction is that it has always been fairly consistent as far as the writing itself goes. It's kept itself in very good form, I think, for about sixty to seventy years. The changes that there have been have been like the swings of the pendulum, but nearly always they've come back to the straight.

SALWAK: What other things have influenced your work?

AIRD: Obviously, if you're a writer, you don't go around with your eyes closed. You become aware of all sorts of influences. You try to make yourself receptive to them rather than anything else, and keep your antennae tuned on as many outside forces as you can, because you're never really quite sure when something's going to come in useful for future works. The most improbable experiences are, in fact, the most likely to be recorded at some later stage for regurgitation in one's fictions.

SALWAK: Did you always want to be a writer?

AIRD: I had originally wanted to be a doctor, not a novelist. In fact, I was on my way to Edinburgh University to read medicine when I suddenly became ill. That was quite a formative influence; I was forced to remain inactive just when I was embarking on my life's work.

SALWAK: Many crime writers have found their medical backgrounds useful adjuncts to their work.

AIRD: Well, the fact that my father was a physician, and that I was brought up living over the shop, so to speak, was a tremendous advantage. Also, by working in a dispensary I became familiar with the properties of all sorts of poisons, of various drugs, and so forth, all of which provided valuable information for a budding crime writer. Then too, you really experience drama when you live in a medical practice. You see life very much up close. You get caught up in other people's domestic dramas, whereas perhaps in the ordinary sense you're not caught up in their anxieties.

SALWAK: Did your writing always come first?

AIRD: Actually, the work of my father's practice, and then of the house, always had priority. Writing was done in the crevices of time left over from one's ordinary duties. I think this is not such a bad thing. Ivory towers are dangerous. You don't see the world from them.

SALWAK: You now live in the small town of Sturry, Canterbury.

AIRD: This has also been an important influence. A village is a confined society, one in which you can isolate both yourself and your fictions. Writing a book requires creating a milieu within which your detective has to operate; he obviously can't take in the whole world. When working from within the village framework or within the closed community of a convent you've got well-defined and easily-understood boundaries beyond which your protagonist only rarely has to venture.

SALWAK: Do your neighbors respect your need for privacy and quiet?

AIRD: I don't have much of either, actually. When you live in a village, you quickly realize that everybody knows everybody else's business. Privacy is defined differently here. But I'm used to that, and it doesn't worry me. My privacy is *not* respected at all and I wouldn't want it to be. I don't know how I should cope if it were. I should be a bit isolated, I think. I've got so used to working in the way in which I do that the fact I live in a village doesn't affect me in the least.

SALWAK: I know you've edited several local histories. What other contributions have you made to village society?

AIRD: I was for nine years or so chairman of the Sturry Parish Council, and that entailed among other things being chairman of the Burial Committee responsible for the administration of the local cemetery. Quite a useful experience for a crime novelist!

SALWAK: What else is there to write about in rural England?

AIRD: Plenty. It's not difficult for any writer to look around England or anywhere else and find things to write about. I don't think people change very much. The differences between the 1960s and 1980s, for example, are really not very noticeable, except in superficial ways. What's so marvelous about writing about human nature is that it doesn't change from one decade to the next. I don't think it matters much whether you're writing about the present day or about Elizabethan England. It's people you are writing about. They never change. The novelist is a mirror of society with a small "s." Society, fashion, and human behavior: reflecting what he sees. I don't think he's an instrument. I think he's just recording events. I see the writer as a mirror reflecting people.

SALWAK: Then how do you view yourself as writer?

AIRD: I see myself as operating entirely within the tradition of English mystery writing. I'm not conscious of moving outside it at all, and if I do, it's certainly unintentional. I don't see my writing as being particularly innovative in any way. Rather, I consciously try to stay within the limits of convention. I think I would agree very much with the title of "I Am a Camera," the play from Christopher Isherwood's novel. I try to record what I see rather than take part in events, in the same way that an artist or a photographer does. The more writing I've done, the more I've come to believe the writer's proper role is to become a camera to life.

SALWAK: What else do you try to accomplish in your fiction?

AIRD: I am trying to delineate the age-old dichotomy between right and wrong. Describing wrong and hoping that right is going to triumph. I think this is one of the reasons that I enjoy detective fiction. It's very clear-cut. I don't mean it to sound high-flown, but I think one is probably writing about good conquering evil in at least one sense. I try to sort out the moral dilemmas of life. With fiction, you can always have one side winning. I don't think it necessarily happens in real life, but it's rather nice to be able to make it happen in your fiction.

SALWAK: Are you saying, then, that your novels provide object lessons for your readers?

AIRD: Well, I'm actually not a moralist at all, but I certainly enjoy writing about detection. The aims of crime fiction are fairly clearcut, and I think this makes for easier writing than in an ordinary novel. You at least have a set framework around which a story can be built, and I find this quite helpful.

SALWAK: Helen MacInnes was often asked, "What's true?" How much is invented?" "Did you experience any of these situations?" How would *you* answer such questions?

AIRD: I don't think any of my writing is necessarily true in the literal meaning of the word. It is meant to be possible. I hope that anything written in any of my books is something that *might* have happened. I don't think any writer can avoid incorporating things that they have noticed. Sloan's philosophy, for instance, is obviously an amalgam of things that have happened to me or that I have heard about or read about or agreed or disagreed with. It obviously hasn't just been plucked out of the air. None of the situations I have written about have actually happened, but I would like to think that any of them could have occurred.

Concerning research, well, all of my books are extensively researched. If I have any doubts about the facts surrounding a story, I look them up. The real danger comes when you think you know something—and don't! As far as actual experiences are concerned, I think in some ways actual events can get in the way of the fiction writer. When you experience something, sometimes you're not able to describe it well after the fact, particularly if it has affected you emotionally.

In one of my books, at the end of *Parting Breath*, there is an escape scene followed by a chase. I was sitting and writing in this quiet room, and I suddenly felt my own pulse quicken as the chase developed beneath my fingertips. How strange! How curious that I could surprise even myself. Obviously, quite a lot of background detail derives from your own experiences—no point living, after all, if you can't use pieces of your own life to make things real. But there's always something extra, something that derives from who knows where.

SALWAK: In a way, then, you're like the actor who, although he is not really Iago, is still somehow able to summon up feelings of rage, jealousy, and hatred.

AIRD: True. You use your mind as a computer. You say, where did I last see that happen, or what was it like when I was in that situation? How precisely did I feel?

SALWAK: Turning specifically to your novels, you were thirty-six when your first novel, *The Religious Body*, was published. This seems a bit later than usual.

AIRD: Actually, I had always done quite a bit of writing on the side.

When I was about thirty, I began asking myself if I was *really* serious about becoming a writer. I decided to get on with it. The idea that everybody should write a book and throw it away has quite a lot to be said for it. So I turned around and wrote two full-length books—one fiction, one nonfiction—neither of which has ever seen the light of day. Subsequently, I wrote a detective story that I didn't think was up to standard. I also suppressed that. It must have had a title, but I honestly can't think of it now, which shouldn't really surprise you from a psychological point of view.

So you can see that I actually wrote quite a bit before the first novel came out. Nobody's ever seen that early work; the manuscripts are literally up in the attic.

SALWAK: Can you tell me something about your first published works?

AIRD: Well, I had written both *The Religious Body* and *The Most Contagious Game* before the former was actually published. And I had already started *The Complete Steel*. I had enough confidence then in my own work that I was relatively well ahead of the game before my first one appeared. *The Religious Body* took about a year to write.

SALWAK: A common theme in your books is the influence of the past on the present. Is this part of your own philosophy?

AIRD: I hadn't actually thought about it in so many words. Perhaps it's part of the writing process. My novels, perhaps all crime novels, are filled with little bits of the past which creep in to the plot as one progresses. It's very difficult to write a crime novel wholly set in the present. Most literary crimes—and criminals—are influenced by what has happened to them in the past; and it's these previous, unseen events which provide the motivations for the murder. That may also be true of real life in a sense. The present often has its roots in the past.

SALWAK: Sloan has been the protagonist, I believe, of all but one of your mystery novels. How did he develop?

AIRD: Strangely enough, I really don't know, and I can't really answer that question except to say that he just seemed to grow of his own accord. In my second novel, *The Most Contagious Game*, I didn't use him because he didn't fit into the plot of that story. Now, of course, I must take public expectations into account.

SALWAK: Sloan is sarcastic at times, yet you obviously feel sympathy for him.

AIRD: That's true, but I'm also trying not to put into Sloan's mouth any words that do not conform to my conceptions of him, which is somebody a little bit sarcastic but not destructively so, just enough to maintain the edge of authority over his subordinates. I try to think of Sloan as the Common Man, oppressed by his superiors, rather defeated by his people working under him. But I see him filling a sort of symbolic role, the working policeman operating against all odds.

SALWAK: Were you surprised at the success of *The Religious Body*?

AIRD: I was very pleased. Nobody who hasn't had it happen can convey to you the great encouragement you get when you send off a book to your publishers, and then so many people write back to tell you how much they enjoyed it. It really does add a lot of power to your will to go on.

SALWAK: But you weren't able to sell the book immediately.

AIRD: No, I sent the manuscript off to three or four publishers who immediately sent it back to me. Then somebody in the business told me that I'd never get anywhere until I got myself a literary agent. So I copied off the rejection letters and sent them to five literary agents in turn, saying, "Am I wasting everybody's time? These are the letters I've had back from the publishers." Four said they were not interested in reading the book, but the fifth wrote back straightaway and said, "Oh yes, I can place this for you." I then had the rather enjoyable experience after the book appeared of having two of the four agents who hadn't bothered to read the book write to me, not realizing, of course, that I was the same person, and offering to act for me. I didn't bother telling them that they'd already rejected it.

SALWAK: How do you get along with your publishers?

AIRD: Very well. I have actually only met my American publisher once, when she came to England. I see my English editor perhaps once every second year. We write, of course. We're on very good terms personally, and I'm very happy with both. I've also had an extremely fruitful relationship with my literary agent. That is important as well.

SALWAK: One of the things I noticed about *The Religious Body* is that while neither Sloan nor Crosby had been to a nunnery, there is a great deal of evidence that the writer had, or that at least she had done her homework.

AIRD: The nunnery that I described was one that I had had tea at on one occasion. In preparing the book I read everything I could find on convents, and used quite a lot of these details for background scenes. I find research itself very tempting. I continually have to tell myself not to confuse research with writing, because doing research is relatively easy when compared with fiction writing. You have to be very careful that you don't spend more time researching than you do writing. I think I could quite happily go on researching forever and never write, which is not the way you finish novels. So I am fairly firm in rationing the amount of research I do, and quite often I will research one book while I am writing another, or alternatively will do what I remember once hearing a humorous writer say, "Write now and research later." So I will often write the novel and then check the facts afterwards. You must never lose sight of the fact that writing is the primary activity.

SALWAK: There's a very interesting epigraph prefacing *The Most Contagious Game*—"For J. D. L., 1900-1965, who was right."

AIRD: J. D. Lewis was a friend of mine who had once been a writer but was in rather poor health when I first began my serious writing, in 1959 or thereabouts. She had done quite a bit of work in her youth, though I don't think I had ever read any of her books. I worked with her co-editing a small quarterly magazine for the Girl Guides. This is how she came to read the book. In fact, she read all of the preliminary chapters of my first two books, and was very helpful in giving me technical advice on layout, manuscript preparation, an appropriate length for chapters and for the book itself, and so forth, all of which was very helpful to a beginner. She was also quite emphatic in telling me over and over again that I would one day find a publisher, which explains my dedication. She had died about a year before the first book came out, so I thought it would be rather nice to acknowledge my debt to her.

SALWAK: *Henrietta Who?* is dedicated to your "eleven o'clock friends."

AIRD: I have four or five friends with whom, on every Saturday morning for I don't know quite how many years—a very, very long time—I have had coffee together. A very informal arrangement. If somebody's free, they come; if not, they don't come. You Americans have a nice word for it, coffee klatch. These are all people who in fact converge on the town on a Saturday morning to do their shopping and things like that, and over the years we have got in the habit of enjoying each other's company.

SALWAK: What sparks your imagination? Character? Setting? The crime itself?

AIRD: All of those things. It varies from book to book. For example, *Henrietta Who?* is about a girl who is summoned home from university to identify the body of her mother, and subsequently told her "mother" had never had a child. This idea was very much sparked off by my reading Rebecca West's book, *The Meaning of Treason*, where she was exploring not so much the psychological but the legal status of people who are stateless. And I started to think, well, suppose I didn't know who I was. How can you be a traitor if you don't know who you are and to which country you owe your allegiance? This was what started me off, postulating a girl who suddenly finds out that she doesn't know who she is.

SALWAK: What about *The Late Phoenix*?

AIRD: That was one of the most interesting books to research. I spent a lot of time in the Imperial War Museum in London. You may remember the classic Harry Dobkin case, who murdered his wife and hoped that she would be mistaken as a blitz victim. She wasn't, of course, and the crime was discovered fairly soon afterwards. But I was just interested to see whether in fact there might still be tucked away somewhere some victim that had not come to light. And I wanted to bring in a little bit of medical background—the doctor's house, the family, the wartime idea of a bird rising again, the phoenix. I think that's what sparked that off—wondering if in fact there weren't another Harry Dobkin down there who hadn't been discovered. I had great fun with an old friend who was a member of the Home Guard, what is now known as Dad's Army. He had kept his .303 rifle, and I had a marvelous afternoon with him lying on the floor of his sitting room pointing it out of the window. He would say, "If you line your sights up, you'll just be able to pick the rector off when he comes around the corner." That feeling of what it was like to handle a rifle...very interesting. I had always heard people tell about what it was like during those times, and I thought it would be interesting to try recording them.

SALWAK: *His Burial Too* differs from the earlier novels quite significantly.

AIRD: As a child I had always loved locked-room mysteries, and I decided that any detective writer worth her salt ought to have a crack at one. I remembered in my younger years going to see Foucault's Pendulum in the Imperial Science Museum. The pendulum demonstrated the rotation of the earth, and I used that as the solution.

SALWAK: *Some Die Eloquent* opens with a bang.

AIRD: It suddenly occurred to me one day that it would be interesting to explore the possibility of somebody dying who had a great deal more money in their possession than anyone expected. Wealth always provides ample motivation for murder.

SALWAK: You seem to have a facility for dialogue.

AIRD: It is enormously satisfying to finish a page of dialogue that you're happy with. You say to yourself, "Ah, this is just as I wanted it to be, not too long, not too short, but just right." I like listening to people talk. I try to keep my ear tuned to the nuances of speech—what they say, how they say it, is quite important. When I hear an interesting phrase, I always make note of it.

SALWAK: *Slight Mourning* represents a new direction in your fiction.

AIRD: The other satisfaction I find in writing comes from exploring a new idea. In *Slight Mourning* I took the idea of paternity, held it up to the light, considered both the scientific and moral sides of the question, and then looked at the implications and ramifications of a murder where it was immaterial whether the husband or wife died. I enjoyed working my way through it. A lot of satisfaction comes from thinking you've covered every aspect of new subject.

SALWAK: Why is this book dedicated to the Girl Guide movement?

AIRD: I had just finished a five-year stint as chairman of the U.K. Finance Committee of the Girl Guide Movement, and then had served a term as assistant treasurer of the World Association of the Girl Guides and Girl Scouts, so I thought it was rather nice to mark the end of a most enjoyable service in that particular way.

SALWAK: *The Body Politic* was written during a difficult time in your life.

AIRD: I made very slow progress on that book, because at that stage I had moved into pretty nearly full-time care of my mother, who was then in her middle eighties and getting extremely frail and unhappy about being left alone for any length of time. As she gradually deteriorated, I found that the entire situation was just not conducive to carrying on with the work. I wrote whenever the opportunity presented itself, but I didn't finish the book, or retype it, until after she'd died. I took me the better half of two and a half years. And in the middle of all this I developed acute pancreatitis, which is extremely painful. I came home from ten days in hospital after having my gallbladder removed and didn't really have much time for convalescence.

SALWAK: There is a very curious scene with a woodpecker....

AIRD: Many, many years ago a member of Parliament used to come give his State of the Nation talk on the veranda overlooking the tennis court, with several hundred people sitting on the lawn listening to him. One year he had just delivered some very, very profound statement about some totally forgotten national matter, and a woodpecker suddenly popped out of the walnut tree and started going, "Ha-ha-ha-*ha*-ha!" This was absolutely devastating. The more solemn the poor man got, the more the bird laughed. It absolutely destroyed the meeting. I always felt it was something that could eventually be used in one of my books. In fact, that part of the politics of *Body Politic* is itself a red herring, for the novel is really about a political body, but in a rather removed sense. A chap comes home unexpectedly from abroad after becoming unwittingly embroiled in an international situation.

SALWAK: *A Dead Liberty* had an interesting genesis.

AIRD: A "liberty" is usually a town with a charter, a royal charter in medieval times. A "dead liberty" is a word we use when somebody has gone a bit far, has encroached in some way, perhaps has borrowed something from you without asking. I was using the title in a different sense, postulating a situation in which, if one chose to remain silent at a trial, certain consequences would follow. In a lot of ways, the justice system requires two people to tango. You have the authorities administering the system, but to a certain degree you must have an acknowledgement on the part of the person being tried that they are taking part in the exercise or charade or whatever.

I thought it would be quite interesting to explore what might happen if somebody remained silent throughout. In fact, I think that if you actually do this in English law, if you persist in your contempt, then you are deemed to have pleaded "not guilty," and the justice system will proceed on that basis. I then created a set of circumstances in which it would be logical for this girl to remain silent, and explored the consequences of that silence. I also incorporated into the book a fairly modern method of murder which hasn't been used very much.

SALWAK: To turn to a different topic, what advice would you give to the aspiring writer?

AIRD: That's difficult. I think just "Keep writing." You do need a certain amount of determination, and I think if you're going to be a writer you go on writing no matter what happens. You plunge through every obstacle.

SALWAK: Can writing be taught?

AIRD: I don't know. I wouldn't like to have to distinguish between what I have learned and what I arrived with, so to speak. I think perhaps everybody needs a little of each. An entirely born novelist who has never learned a thing is as daunting a prospect as somebody who has not got any talent but is prepared to learn everything.

SALWAK: Do you read your critics?

AIRD: With great interest. If they all make the same point, I take note of it.

SALWAK: Do you ever stop and think how many readers you have?

AIRD: I don't even know how many copies of my books are around. I don't have a specific reader in mind at all. I concentrate entirely on Inspector Sloan.

SALWAK: What is a typical day for you?

AIRD: I try to work first thing in the morning, and I usually come downstairs and start straightaway, before I look at the post or the paper and get caught up in the day. At least until nine, and always armed with a large pot of tea. I'm always full of resolve that I'm going to come back and do a bit more later in the day, and some days I do. On others I do associated things—researching, reading, clerical work.

SALWAK: You have been quoted as saying there is a great deal of similarity between having a baby and having a book.

AIRD: The most striking thing to me is that somewhere round about the halfway stage I get a most definite quickening which is similar to what comes halfway through pregnancy. I can't really describe it better than that. There is a moment about halfway through when I suddenly get the feeling that the book's come alive, and that I'm on the downward stretch to finishing it. It's a very nice feeling indeed.

SALWAK: Do you often revise?

AIRD: Actually, I revise as I write. I try to get each page complete as it is before going on to the next, even though I may go through it a half dozen times. Then when that page is finished I very seldom go back again, just very occasionally. Unlike some writers, I don't do a rough draft of the book and then a better draft and then a better draft still. I start on page one and keep to page one until I'm happy with page one, and then on to page two. It's always been that way.

SALWAK: What's your average daily output?

AIRD: About three hundred words a day.

SALWAK: Then how many months does it usually take you to write a book?

AIRD: Usually nine months to a year. *A Late Phoenix* took me a much longer time to research, and it obviously needed it. But generally speaking, I don't spend a great deal of time on research, just as little as I feel I ought to, to get the facts straight.

SALWAK: Do you have an outline in mind when you begin a book?

AIRD: I just sit down with an idea or a situation, and explore it as I go along. I am quite happy to start Chapter One without knowing much of what's going to happen.

SALWAK: Do you usually type the first draft of one of your books?

AIRD: I handwrite, a few pages on legal-sized pink sheets, in blue ink, three or four pages at a time, and then retype them.

SALWAK: Do your characters ever surprise you?

AIRD: Occasionally. They sometimes suddenly come out and do

something unexpected. You see, I'm not an autobiographical writer. In fact, I try consciously not to do that, but to work primarily from the imagination and not to bring in elements from my life. Consequently, my characters will sometimes spring little surprises on me.

SALWAK: Do your friends ever recognize themselves in your novels?

AIRD: I have friends who have said so on occasion, but I am not conscious of having put them there. Even when a similarity is pointed out to me, I can't see that I've described them at all.

On the other hand, I do have a friend who is always coming across little things that she has *said* in my books, because I like to copy bits of dialogue here and there. She's one of those people who have a very good talent for making astringent comments. So quite often I do in fact consciously write down and retain some of her comments for reuse elsewhere. But not her character.

SALWAK: I also enjoy your chapter headings.

AIRD: In one recent book, I took the heads from the Office of Compline, which is very interesting indeed. I'd read through the service and found some lovely sayings, like "Before the Ending of the Day," "A Perfect End," "Beware of thy Adversary, the Devil," "Brethren Be Sober, Be Vigilant." I've got one or two other improbable sources of chapter headings that I perhaps will not tell you about until the next book. It's great fun. It's nice when you come to the end of a chapter, when you're looking back for a little bit of relaxation, and can say, "Ah, now I'll pick out a nice heading for the next chapter."

SALWAK: How do you usually end a chapter?

AIRD: I break them somewhere between 3,100 and 4,000 words, and try to end them on a note that definitely constitutes some termination or completion. If I have got two equally good endings, I'll try to move them around so that each actually ends a chapter, instead of one coming right after the other. I think these little details are very important to the reader, and I go out of my way to construct them carefully.

SALWAK: Are you healthier for writing?

AIRD: Actually, I'm not very healthy at all. I think probably I write in spite of not being very healthy rather than because of it. I've never been one not to have some work on hand.

SALWAK: Would you enjoy serving as a writer-in-residence?

AIRD: That would be rather fun to do. It's something I would enjoy, I think, although I don't know anything much about the younger generation. I don't know how'd they react.

SALWAK: Do you have any unfulfilled literary ambitions? What is your greatest satisfaction in writing?

AIRD: I would like to write a play very much, a three-act play. To me, I find the greatest satisfaction in writing the last few words of a book and finishing it, and I tend to switch off after that point. Rather like having a baby and having it adopted immediately. As far as I'm concerned, when I've finished the book, the last page of the last chapter, and have sent it to my agent, I've really switched off. I read it again once for proofreading, and I've never read any of them again after that. Sometimes it's a great effort of will to recall a book that one's written twelve or fifteen years ago. There's a definite feeling with each one that this is over and done with.

SALWAK: Your career has been a graded one, hasn't it?

AIRD: Yes, and I'm very grateful for that. I've been very lucky, and I'm very thankful that it has been a slow progression. An overnight bestseller would probably have terrified me. It's very difficult to write a book after that kind of experience. If you're inching your way forward, I think you do better as a writer. At any rate, this suits my sort of writing better, and it suits me better, too.

SELECTED SECONDARY BIBLIOGRAPHY

Aldrich, Pearl G. "Aird, Catherine," in *Twentieth-Century Crime and Mystery Writers, Second Edition*, edited by John M. Reilly. New York: St. Martin's Press, 1985, cloth, p. 7-8.

Herbert, Rosemary. "Is There Still an English Cozy Mystery? in *MD* (May, 1986): 94-95.

Jacobson, Jeanne M. "Catherine Aird's Comfortable Corpus," in *The Drood Review of Mystery* 111 (November, 1983): 3-5.

Koontz, Dean R. "Catherine Aird," in *How to Sell Bestselling Fiction*. London: Popular Press, 1981, cloth, p. 278.

A P. D. JAMES CHRONOLOGY

1920 Phyllis Dorothy James born August 3rd at Wexford, England.

1931 Educated at Cambridge Girls' High School (through 1937).

1939 Works during World War II as a Red Cross nurse and at the Ministry of Food (through 1944).

1941 Marries Ernest C. B. White, by whom she has two daughters.

1949 Serves as Principal Administrative Assistant, North West Regional Hospital Board, London (through 1968).

1962 James's first novel, *Cover Her Face*, is published in England by Faber & Faber (U.S. edition, 1966).

1963 *A Mind to Murder* published in Britain (U.S. edition, 1967).

1964 James's husband, Ernest White, dies.

1967 Third novel, *Unnatural Causes*, published. Receives Crime Writers Association award.

1968 "Moment of Power" published in *Ellery Queen's Mystery Magazine*, and receives an award. Works as a Senior Civil Servant for the Home Office, Criminal and Police Departments (through 1972).

1971 Publishes *Shroud for a Nightingale*, the fourth Dalgliesh novel, and *The Maul and the Pear Tree* (with Thomas A. Critchley), a study of the Radcliffe Highway murders. Receives an Edgar Award for Best Novel from Mystery Writers of America and a Silver Dagger from the Crime Writers Association (U.K.).

1972 *An Unsuitable Job for a Woman*, featuring a new detective, Cordelia Gray, published (U.S. edition, 1973). Receives a second Edgar Award. Works as a Principal for the Home Office, Criminal Police Department (through 1979).

1975 Publishes *The Black Tower*, which receives a Silver Dagger Award.

1977 *Death of an Expert Witness* published.

1979 Becomes Justice of the Peace for Willesden District, London.

1980 *Innocent Blood* published.

1982 Publishes *The Skull Beneath the Skin*.

1983 Made an Officer of the Order of the British Empire by Queen Elizabeth II.

1985 Becomes a Fellow of the Institute of Hospital Administrators, and Chairman of the Society of Authors.

1986 Publishes *A Taste for Death* (U.S. edition, 1987).

1989 *Devices and Desires*, the author's eleventh novel, published (U.S. edition, 1990).

P. D. James
(photo by Jerry Bauer)

II.
AN INTERVIEW WITH
P. D. JAMES

SALWAK: To what do you attribute your appetite for crime fiction?

JAMES: This is a difficult question, because I sometimes suspect that the answer may lie very deep in the roots of personality, and I'm wary about getting involved in, as it were, psychological discussions, simply because I'm not a psychologist. But I do wonder, really whether this, not exactly an obsession—I think your word "appetite" is better—for writing about crime, may not be one way one has of sublimating certain emotions, whether I may not be basically frightened of violence and, indeed, possibly of death. And this is one way of trying to deal with these irrational fears. Because in real life I do find violence very frightening, and murder I regard as the ultimate crime, the one for which you can never make reparation.

So why do I want to write about it? I don't think I know. I think there may have been in my very early life some emotional trauma or insecurity, and this is one way of trying to construct a world in which there is an ultimate answer to problems that may otherwise seem unacceptable or insoluble. I'm not really sure.

On the easier level, of course, I do take pleasure in constructing a novel. I'm not interested in writing books which are short exercises in sensibility, which seem to begin and end for no particular reason. The novelists I most enjoy have written well-constructed fictions, so that there are a number of technical reasons why I find the mystery a fascinating kind of book to write. But the psychological reasons, why I should be so absorbed in the treatment of death, I think are more difficult.

SALWAK: In *Innocent Blood*, Philippa, an aspiring novelist herself, thinks, "The artist should suffer in childhood trauma without breaking." Do you believe that?

JAMES: I think I do believe that. I feel that very often the best writing, the best artistic endeavor, does result from early trauma or early unhappiness. I don't know that I have a great deal of evidence that I can immediately deduce, and I accept that my own childhood wasn't unhappy or deprived by the standards of most human beings. Those of us who are lucky enough to be born into the prosperous Western world forget that, for most of the human race, childhood is a matter of fear and hunger. We suffer a little, and feel that we are unfortunate. Obviously, simply by virtue of being born into the society I was born into, I was a privileged human being. I didn't have to remember it. But nevertheless, I do look back on childhood as a time of some strain, and I think that had I enjoyed an absolutely happy one, without any strain, I would have been less inclined to write. Writing is a compulsion; it is a need of the personality.

SALWAK: Whom did you enjoy reading as a child and as you grew up, particularly in the detective genre?

JAMES: Oh, Dorothy L. Sayers was a very potent influence when I was a girl. I obviously read in the genre, but I'm not addicted to it, in the sense that I have to have my daily fix. I read Conan Doyle, of course, and the classics in the genre when I was young. I suppose Margery Allingham, to an extent, was an influence. And I admire her very much as a writer. It's interesting that it is the women that I prefer. I have a great admiration for the American private eye, the hard-boiled school. I think Dashiell Hammett and Raymond Chandler were very good writers indeed, and their influence has been significant—not only on their own genre, but on the craft of the novelist generally. But for my own relaxation and pleasure I like the more gentle, English classical school. As I often say, "malice domestic." Or to paraphrase Rupert Brooke, "stands the church clock at ten to three, and is there arsenic still for tea?" Was it Auden who said, in one of his essays, that the body must be doubly shocking not only because it's a corpse but because of where it is? A corpse on the drawing room floor is far more potent a symbol than a dozen riddled corpses down the mean city street, and so it is for me.

SALWAK: You mentioned Dorothy L. Sayers. In one of your essays about her, you wrote, "By the time she wrote *Gaudy Night,* Miss Sayers, like her alter ego [Harriet Vane], had become dangerously enamored of her aristocratic sleuth." Is that a potential hazard for the female writer, and are there other hazards as well?

JAMES: I don't think I'm in any danger of falling in love with my sleuth, but I feel there is a danger with some women writers, in that we rather tend to glamorize or romanticize our heroes, that they tend to be a little too perfect. I'm always aware of this danger. With Adam Dalgliesh, I have tried to create a man whose qualities I admire. I mean, obviously I have admiration for his qualities, because if you're going to keep one character going through a series of books you must admire at least some of his qualities; otherwise, the whole thing will become totally boring. One just couldn't settle down to have a series of books that had a detective one hated and disliked.

Although I think it's interesting that in some of Agatha Christie's books she has this Ariadne Oliver, a woman crime writer with a Swedish detective. Whether Agatha Christie was speaking for herself, I don't know, but certainly she suggested in these books that Hercule Poirot had become an absolute millstone. She hated him and wished she'd never invented him. But I certainly don't feel that way about Adam Dalgliesh, although I do have to remind myself there are things about his character which I don't admire. He's so completely detached at times, even a little cold, that I wouldn't have thought him easy to work for at all.

SALWAK: He occasionally makes mistakes, too, doesn't he? At times he does *not* solve the crime, at times his hunches *are* proved wrong.

JAMES: Yes, as I think in real life they would be, for any police official.

SALWAK: He *isn't* perfect.

JAMES: He is *not* perfect, and I think he'd be boring if he were. He can be unkind in his own way, though I don't think he intends to be. As I say, not an easy man to work for, and certainly a perfectionist and a loner.

SALWAK: How did Adam's character develop? Was he solidly in your mind from the start, or just an accidental creation? I know that his character develops as we move from one novel to the next, and yet he remains essentially the same person. He learns, he grows in stature as a man and as a detective. But how did it all begin?

JAMES: I'm happy you think he grows in stature as both man and detective. I certainly intended that he should.

Well, he didn't begin entirely by chance. When I set out to write my first crime novel, this was one of the most important and almost the earliest decision that had to be made. Am I going to have a private eye? Or am I going to have a professional policeman? Of course, the English tradition is very much for the omniscient private eye who makes rings around the professional police force, from Sherlock Holmes onwards.

But I did want to write a fairly realistic novel. I know that's begging all sorts of questions: can one write a realistic murder story when the difference between real police work and fictional police work is, and has to be, considerable? I wanted to at least create the illusion of a real world, and it seemed to me that I ought, therefore, to have a professional police officer, because in real life private individuals just don't keep stumbling over bodies. Even if they did, their chances of carrying out a successful murder investigation are very slight.

Also, the police officer has the backup facilities of the force available to him, and an excuse for getting continually involved. It struck me that the dangers were that one would create a rather stereotyped, even dull character. If you choose to have a private eye you can create one of either sex; my private eye is a girl, as you know, Cordelia Gray. And you can give your private eye quite an interesting job in real life. You could have somebody who was a writer or a painter or an actor. I think this adds considerably to the interest.

I decided that in this case, since I wanted to make him more sensitive than the usual idea of a policeman, that he would be a poet. From those small beginnings the character developed, and continues to develop, I hope. But I didn't want him to be too much in the tradition of the perfect, English, upper-class gent, which I think is a danger in my kind of mystery. I placed him socially rather in the middle grade, as the son of a country rector. I mean, he's obviously well-educated, but he's not a sprig of aristocracy.

SALWAK: *Innocent Blood* is, of course, an "odd one out," in that Adam does not appear at all, and in *An Unsuitable Job for a Woman* he is not directly involved in the case, but he does work "behind the scenes," so to speak. *Is* detective work an unsuitable job for a woman?

JAMES: I should have thought it was a very suitable job indeed. I think that the police forces would be well advised to make far more use of women, particularly intelligent women, in the upper echelons of the detective ranks. Women are very good at knowing when someone else is lying, particularly another woman. And I think men in some respects are much more liable to confide in a woman than they are in a man. There's a great body of unused talent for detection. Also, women have such an eye for detail. It astounds me that in nearly all of the world's police forces, the upper ranks are predominantly male. Some women would certainly excel there.

SALWAK: This might help explain why so many respectable English women are so good at writing about murder.

JAMES: I think so. Their eye for detail is certainly significant and important. With this type of book—as I say, the "malice domestic"—the scene is nearly always set in a fairly normal, ordinary setting. In fact, one of the attractions of such fiction is the contrast between ordinary life and the appalling contamination of crime. Clue-making does demand an eye for detail, for the minutiae of everyday living. Who would have worn that extraordinary shade of purple lipstick? Who did take a last drink out of that poisoned cup? Who prepared the lettuce salad dressing? Where were people present at any particular time?

Also, I think the emotions of the characters are tremendously important. A book would have no interest for me—no novel has any interest—unless one is actually involved in the emotions of the characters. That's really basically what fiction is about. And I think that women are particularly interested in those strong emotions which can result in murder, especially in the closed community, where there can be jealousies, resentments, and dislikes constantly festering away. That's probably our *forte*, the immense mysteriousness of human nature.

SALWAK: Which are more difficult for you to write about, men or women?

JAMES: They're equally difficult. There are problems in writing about men, but I think it would be the same for a man writing about women. It's clothes, really. I don't think it's emotions. I mean, I may be totally wrong, but I feel that I can understand the male way of thinking. I don't see why this should be so drastically different from a female way of thinking and feeling. But it's what it feels like in the morning to be a male putting on your clothes. Perhaps that's why in my books my readers are often told what women are wearing in far more detail than they are told what men are wearing.

SALWAK: As a writer, then, is your first duty to yourself—or to your readers?

JAMES: Oh, to your own talent, of course, and I suppose that means to yourself: to do the best that you can, with what you can do, hoping very much that your readers will like it. Often with a mystery what readers are hoping for, in a sense, is a little relaxation, a little vicarious excitement, an escape from the problems and difficulties of ordinary life. That is no doubt one of the reasons why people like crime fiction. I don't think providing that escape is an ignoble aim. It is the same with people who can write funny books. I think P. G. Wodehouse has done more for human happiness than a great many far more serious novelists—a great deal more. Basically every writer, if he's a serious writer, is trying to satisfy himself and his own talent.

SALWAK: It's obvious that you enjoy your work. I wonder, however, whether you are consciously aware of drawing from trends in "mainstream fiction" as you work on a crime novel.

JAMES: This is one of the things that I'm in fact trying to do, that I'm aiming to do. I like the constraints of the genre. Obviously I wouldn't go on with it if I didn't. But I am trying, I think, within those constraints, to write a book which has claims to be regarded as a serious novel. I know I've said that over and over again, but it still remains true. If another plot or idea presented itself to me as strongly as did the idea for *Innocent Blood*, I can see that I would write another novel which would move outside the constraints as that book did.

Although I think that *Innocent Blood* does show evidence of what I have learned from writing crime novels. It seems to be a natural progression from the genre, particularly in the way the action and the internal tensions of the novel are dealt with. I would be very happy to write another book which moved outside the strict conventions of the mystery. But I must admit it would almost certainly be a novel that would be in some way still a crime novel. It might not be a detective story. There does seem to be this need to deal with people at the extremity of emotion.

SALWAK: *Innocent Blood* must have been an exciting book for you to write.

JAMES: It was. It was also a very exhausting one to write, and very traumatic. I was immensely excited by the plot and by the characters. I think you're right: in a sense there was material in the book for a half a dozen novels. There's a novel in the relationship of the adopting couple. There's a novel certainly in the relation of the girl and the love affair with her father, apart from the crime aspect of the story. It is a very clotted novel, a very dense novel, emotionally. I was very excited by the whole idea. It's interesting—I hate to use the word "challenging," because that's such an overworked word, but I suppose that's the most accurate one: to tackle something outside the genre, to see if I could do it to my own satisfaction. It seemed to have been done to the satisfaction of critics, by and large. But one does work primarily for one's own approbation, and I was pleased with the end result.

SALWAK: What sparked your imagination with *Innocent Blood*?

JAMES: Well, it was very interesting, because there were two events, one very far distant and one fairly recent, and they came together. It was an example of how something that happens deep in the past is rooted in one's subconscious and begins to sprout when the moment comes. The very distant event was a real-life murder case here. Twenty years or more ago, when we still had the death penalty, a young husband whose wife had just given birth to their first child visited her in the nursing home the day after the baby was born. On his way home he called in on his parents-in-law—their name was Goodman—and battered them to death with a television aerial. He was a very inexpert murderer, because he had blood on his clothes, and then he went home and tried to burn his suit in the boiler. The police recovered it with a lot of additional forensic evidence. He was convicted and hanged.

At that time my thoughts were so centered on this newborn child because I thought, "What is his mother going to say to him when he asks where his father is, or how he died, or when he asks them about his grandparents?" How do you say to your child, "you haven't any grandparents on the maternal side because your father killed them both and was hanged himself?" If you try to change your name, sooner or later somebody's going to tell him, and what effect is it going to have on him? So I suppose all those thoughts got absorbed or buried in my subconscious.

Then there came an act of Parliament here which for the first time gave adopted adults—that is, from the age of eighteen—the right to have copies of their original birth certificates. This did in fact break faith with a lot of people who had given their children up for adoption or had received children for adoption, on the understanding that there would be complete secrecy both ways. Parliament, therefore, in the way that Parliament does, rather salved its conscience by saying that young people had to go to a social work counselor—social workers having replaced priests as the secular ministers of our society. But I think Parliament was probably right in deciding that the need of young people to know their roots ought to outweigh other considerations. I'm not criticizing the legislation. I think it was probably good. But it was these two ideas that came together.

I thought, "Well, what are some of these young people going to find out? Suppose some young woman had managed to fabricate for herself a world in which she lived satisfactorily and which was completely overthrown. How would she deal with that?" It could have been used as the basis for an orthodox detective story, because it would make a very good motive for murder: some people might want her to be put out of the way before she could find out the truth of her parentage. I thought it was too strong a plot for that treatment. I wanted to explore other aspects of the theme, like the search for identity and the growth of human love, and even the old argument about whether nurture or heredity is dominant. There are so many themes. So it was a very exciting book to write.

SALWAK: Isn't it true that many children go through a period in their lives when they wonder whether or not they really belong to their parents?

JAMES: Do you know, I believe so. People say this is very very common indeed—that children do wonder whether they are their parents' child. And some like to make little pretences to themselves that they were once adopted.

SALWAK: And then at some period and for some reason, they find assurance that their parents are indeed who they say they are.

JAMES: I wonder if this is one expression of the basic insecurity and trauma of early life. You can come from a very privileged background and still have trauma, and it seems to me inseparable from childhood. This feeling of being a changeling may be an expression of great anxiety. I'm not really their child, they may reject me. I've got to sort of live up to some kind of ideal. This is what Philippa felt in *Innocent Blood*.

SALWAK: *Innocent Blood* wasn't the original title, was it?

JAMES: Well, I had great trouble with that title. Titles are interesting, aren't they? Sometimes the title is so natural, seems so right and inevitable: *Shroud for a Nightingale,* for example, seemed to be a right title—once I knew that I was going to set it in a nurse training school. *Innocent Blood* was originally called *The Blood Tie,* but then very late, long after the novel was written and submitted, my editors discovered that somebody had used that title. Then we had *Blood Relations*—but somebody had used that. Then we were in a desperate state. I was delighted with the change in the end. It came as kind of inspiration. We were having cross-Atlantic telephone calls, and when you get into this kind of difficulty you can find yourself suggesting extraordinarily odd titles. My editor at Faber was desperately looking through a book of quotations for anything that might come to light. Then I went to bed, and when I woke up in the morning it just came through my mind: *Innocent Blood*. I think it is a very good title, far better than *The Blood Tie*.

SALWAK: In that novel you make very clear the reasons for murder, psychological and otherwise. But is there a general answer you might give to the question, "Why does someone murder"?

JAMES: Many domestic murders are committed because someone is at the end of their endurance, have had more than they can take. But of course that in law would almost certainly be construed as manslaughter. The number of murderers, at least in this country, who undertake deliberately premeditated murder are, thank God, a fairly small group of people. And that's what murder is—premeditated, "the willful killing of another human being living under the Queen's peace with malice aforethought, expressed or implied."

I suppose what I'm saying is that nearly all of us are capable of killing another human being, given the right circumstances or provocation. I'm sure I could kill in defense of my own children; I'm sure I would in defense of my own life, if it's a question of he's coming to get me, do I get him first? This seems to be natural, almost instinctive. But deliberately to sit down and to think, "I'm going to get rid of him—or her"—that I know I couldn't do. I think very few of us can.

And, of course, you still have to make the obvious subdivision between those who have rational knowledge of what they're doing and those who are mentally disturbed. This is a very, very difficult question. It seems to me, nowadays, that if people do something that is outrageously wicked we automatically say, "Well, they are mentally disturbed." I mean, they may have been living perfectly ordinary, successful lives before the killing with no signs of being mentally disturbed at all. But if they do something which is horrible and evil, we assume that he couldn't have been in his right mind to do that. And that leads us to the whole question of personal responsibility, a terribly difficult one. So I suppose that's the answer. We're all capable of killing, but thank God we are not all capable of deliberate murder.

SALWAK: I recall reading a review of *Crime and Punishment* in which the writer offered that Dostoevsky must have killed, for he had rendered so realistically the murders of the two elderly ladies. Dostoevsky's retort was, "How do you know it's real?"

JAMES: It's a very clever response, isn't it? Because one is always getting that question. I know that with *The Black Tower*, which starts off with Dalgliesh getting a reprieve from what he sees as a death sentence (he thought that he had leukemia, but he hadn't), one of my readers wrote to me that she found this passage very moving, and that I myself must have been in the situation of fearing that I had a fatal illness and of having been reprieved. I'm thankful to say I've not had a serious illness, I haven't experienced what Dalgliesh experienced.

This is what being a writer is, isn't it? That is, having the creative imagination which enables you to enter into feelings, into emotions which you haven't actually experienced yourself. I suppose there has to be some basis at least for the exercise of this ability. If I'm ill, I'm quite ready to believe that it's the symptom of something absolutely frightening. We must all have experienced that. I suppose you just build on that. What would you feel like if in fact your worst suspicions were confirmed? But it is interesting to hear some readers say that since one of my characters expresses a particular opinion that I myself must share it. I think in *Innocent Blood* Philippa says that Scase has the mind of the crime writer, obsessed with trivia. Do I feel that way about crime writers?

SALWAK: Your novels do have a solidity of facts. Your work with the crime division and earlier with the hospital must help to account for that.

JAMES: Particularly my work in the hospital service, oddly enough, because three novels arose from this—*Shroud for a Nightingale, Mind to Murder,* and also *The Black Tower.*

SALWAK: Yes, to read about a murder that involved the handicapped was new to me.

JAMES: Some people found that very difficult to take. It's quite a black book, that; in some ways it's as dark a book as *Innocent Blood*.

SALWAK: Are hospitals really as oppressive and rule-bound as you've depicted them in *Shroud for a Nightingale?*

JAMES: I doubt whether they are now. There's been a great sort of loosening. But I think they were then. Today student nurses are treated with a great deal more consideration and enjoy much easier living conditions than they did during my generation. And yet people often go into hospital and they come out and say, "Well, in the old days, the system would have never put up with that." I think discipline is a difficult thing, because you are dealing with life and death, in which mistakes can kill people. If it all gets too happy-go-lucky, I think there could be a drop in standards. It's rather the same as running a ship of war. You want a happy ship, but it's still a fighting community. You've got to have some discipline to cope with the battle against death and disease.

SALWAK: I enjoy the fact that one of Dalgliesh's books of poetry, I think his most recent, is found on the bookshelf next to the murdered nurse. You must have great fun with little touches like that.

JAMES: I do, yes; I do have fun.

SALWAK: Or his relationship with Deborah, until she leaves for New York.

JAMES: Sometimes people ask what happened to Deborah. Maybe in my next book I must resurrect Deborah.

SALWAK: Deborah finally grows impatient with Dalgliesh, doesn't she?

JAMES: Yes indeed, and this is what I mean by his not being too perfect. He would claim when the affair ended that the job must come first. But I knew that it wasn't the job that was coming first; he just didn't want to be emotionally involved. He just wanted a life in which he could have an attractive mistress who wouldn't make demands on him or his job. I think I made the point that that's what he liked about the job—the excuse for being private, not committed. And he obviously has the ability to solve a case without worrying too greatly about what happens afterwards.

SALWAK: Your first novel, *Cover Her Face,* was written in part because you had to support your daughters. But it seems a very workmanlike job indeed, very polished. I wonder if there is any appreciable body of writing before that from which you learned your craft?

JAMES: No, there wasn't any body of work, at least nothing that was ever completed. I think it's not completely true to say that I had to do it to help support the children, because I didn't honestly feel that writing would do much to support my family. That is why I found myself a safe job in the health service. I thought, "I've got to have a check coming in once a month." Of course, if the writing did make money, that was going to be jam on the bread. But I honestly don't think I expected that it would make much, I suppose partly because one is brought up to expect that it's difficult to get a first novel published, and that when it does, you're not going to make a fortune. Those seemed not to be the days, too, of the immediate bestseller.

My kind of orthodox detective story, although very popular, isn't usually the sort of book which immediately becomes a bestseller and makes a fortune. It was really that I did know from the first that I was a writer. I felt that despite the difficulties, if I didn't get on and write, I was going to be a failure. It was no good thinking that there would be a time when the job would be easier, when I wouldn't have to take professional examinations, or when my husband might get better and the children would be older. When those times came there would be other problems, other difficulties. So I *had* to settle down and write my first novel. I obviously hoped very much that it would be published, and that it would be liked, but I'm sure the need is to write for your own satisfaction—for your *ego* satisfaction, really.

SALWAK: Was your first novel difficult to write?

JAMES: It was, because I was doing a great deal of reading to get myself qualified for a professional examination in hospital administration, and was visiting my husband in hospital. My children were home for holidays, too. The plotting and the writing went on for two and a half to three years. It's interesting that one of the reviewers said that it was difficult to see this as a first novel. I think it may simply be because I didn't start very young. Possibly had I started at eighteen or nineteen, I should have had to go through the usual disheartening process of rejection slips time and again. I'm not sure I would have had the courage to do that.

SALWAK: And in that first novel there were signs of so much more to come.

JAMES: Things have developed, yes. I'm astounded how many people put *Cover Her Face* among their favorites, because to me it is so much a first novel. Although I can see the signs of development, it's so traditional—a country house murder. It's almost as if I'd set out to do a *pastiche* of the genre. But people do like it.

SALWAK: But then one might say that every crime writer worth her salt should write a country house murder.

JAMES: Well, Auden said he couldn't bear to read a detective story mystery that wasn't set in an English village.

SALWAK: In your second novel, *A Mind to Murder*, there is the following statement: "How long could you stay detached before you lose your own soul?" That's a prominent theme in your work, isn't it?

JAMES: It is a theme in my work, yes, but it's also a theme in C. P. Snow's novels. I think one of his characters saw that there's great dignity in being an observer, but that if you do it long enough, you are in danger of losing your soul—or something like that. My character, Adam Dalgliesh, for example—if he just studies other people almost as if they are biological specimens and rejects any real personal commitment to another person, that can be dangerous to him as a human being.

SALWAK: What about the writer? Is that true as well?

JAMES: Oh yes, I think it can be. Someone once said that writers have a slice of ice in their hearts, and I certainly can see how that's true, both for writers and artists. Possibly that's why some of them have difficulties in their private relations. In my novel *The Skull Beneath the Skin,* my character says something like that towards the end of the book. If you distance yourself from all human concerns, you distance yourself from human pity.

SALWAK: Dalgliesh doesn't appear in that book, does he?

JAMES: Only just by a mention. It's another Cordelia Gray story. My faithful readers wanted Cordelia back, and this was a plot which was very suitable for her. *The Skull Beneath the Skin* is very much a return to the traditional English detective story.

SALWAK: I understand that your third novel, *Unnatural Causes,* was inspired by a scene at Dunwich.

JAMES: It is a most extraordinary place, really. It was a great seaport in medieval times, but now there are all these churches, graveyards under the sea. And all that remains is a deserted and desolate hamlet. I have a cottage very near, so I know that part of the east coast, and I was so influenced by its atmosphere that I knew I would have to set a novel there. Setting is tremendously important to me. Very often it is the setting that sparks off my creative imagination.

SALWAK: *Shroud for a Nightingale* includes a particularly ingenious method of murder.

JAMES: This again was an idea that lay very deep in the subconscious. In the war I did some Red Cross nursing—that must have been 1939, twenty years before the novel was written—and as part of my training we watched a volunteer nurse being fed by a tube which she swallowed into her stomach. I wasn't on the receiving end or on the pushing-down-the-tube end, fortunately. Perhaps this is an example of the morbid imagination of the crime novelist, because at the time and long before I had written my first novel, I thought: "Well, yes, there they are pouring down this warmed milk, but suppose it wasn't warmed milk, but it was lethal disinfectant. What a way of getting rid of someone." So when I thought I'd like to set a novel in a nurse training school, there was the ready-made death at hand. So in *Shroud for a Nightingale,* it was a mixture of the setting and the method of murder which provided inspiration, whereas in *Unnatural Causes* it was the setting only.

SALWAK: In that same novel, there is the sentence, "Murder was frequently the last resort of the unintelligent." That is certainly true.

JAMES: Oh indeed, in real life, yes. Violence, anyway, is frequently the last resort of the unintelligent.

SALWAK: And the violence in *An Unsuitable Job for a Woman* involves Cordelia Gray directly, and Dalgliesh only indirectly. Why did you use Cordelia?

JAMES: I wanted to set a novel in Cambridge, which is a city I love. I wanted the story to take place in summer, the golden summer days in Cambridge. I suppose I could have sent Dalgliesh to Cambridge, but the difficulty is, of course, if you're trying to write a realistic crime novel, that the provincial forces—I'm not sure if this is exactly the same in other countries—are perfectly competent to handle their own murders. In the mysteries written in the 1930s you always called the Yard, but now it's very rare in real detection that the Yard is called in. Certainly Dalgliesh wouldn't have been called in to go down to Cambridge to investigate the hanging of an ex-student, and of course it wasn't even an official murder. I had this idea of a rather seedy detective agency and the relationship between the girl and the dead proprietor. So again, it was the idea of the place and the character together. I liked writing that book. It was probably the easiest and in many ways the most purely pleasurable of my books to write.

SALWAK: I notice that most of your victims are unsympathetic characters. Why?

JAMES: Well, in a sense I suppose they have to be. If people are generous and pleasant and courageous and likable, they are seldom surrounded by a group of people with strong reasons for getting rid of them. So nearly always the victim is difficult, to put it mildly.

But however difficult, disagreeable, hateful, even dangerous or evil the victims may be, they are still, or should be in the book, real human beings with credible reasons for being as they are. It has always seemed to me that the character of the victim is as important as the character of the detective or the suspect. If you don't create a real human being with whom people can to some extent sympathize, how are they going to care whether he's killed or how he's killed or why he was killed?

SALWAK: In *Death of an Expert Witness*, there is the line, "It was the strangest part of a detective's job, this building up of a relationship with the dead. Once dead, he is then subject of psychological interest." Do you find this to be true for the writer as well as the detective, and how does this relate to your methods of writing?

JAMES: Very much so. Before writing I have to be absolutely certain about the main line of the novel. And I have to know where it's going to be set, who is going to be killed, why he's going to be killed, who the chief suspects are, what their motives are, how the crime is going to be detected, and the way in which I'm going to deal with the *dénouement*. But I need a great deal more than that. I need to think about the story for a very long time before I begin writing it; but when the moment comes when I feel it's just right, I can begin writing. By then I will have set down the action in chart form, but I don't begin at the beginning and go through. I might begin with the last chapter, or I might begin by writing some passage of dialogue between two of the characters. And finally it is pieced together. Writing for me is rather what I imagine shooting a film is. You see it in scenes, you see it in situations, you see it through different viewpoints, and just as the filmmaker must, you take advantage of certain lights and certain weather in certain locations. So I take advantage of my own states of emotion. Sometimes I'm more ready to write one scene or another, dialogue or action or description. And finally the complete novel is put together.

SALWAK: Several of your novels have now been filmed.

JAMES: Yes, *Innocent Blood* was done by Twentieth Century-Fox, and over here Anglia Television shot *Death of an Expert Witness*, *Shroud for a Nightingale*, and several others.

SALWAK: Dalgliesh admires Jane Austen, and, I suspect, so does the author.

JAMES: I've always admired her, she's always been my favorite novelist, and I do see an influence on my writing. It's interesting that I read her when I was very young, because people say that Jane Austen is not a young person's writer. But I was immediately enchanted by her and have been reading and re-reading her all my life. Her delicate irony, the detachment, the construction—those are the attractions for me. But I think it's very difficult to know really precisely where the attraction lies. I suspect she's a novelist's novelist. But I can see others who are more recent influences in my work—Dorothy L. Sayers, Evelyn Waugh, and Graham Greene.

SALWAK: You're frequently "packaged" in the U.S. as the new Agatha Christie. How do you react to that?

JAMES: I just think it's inaccurate at best. I mean, I can see the reason for doing this: Dame Agatha is dead, and perhaps publishers need someone to succeed her. Of course, one couldn't hope to achieve her phenomenal financial success. I think that it's very difficult to explain the universality of her appeal. She was preeminently a fabricator of ingenious plots. This is where her strength lay. And of course she is immensely readable, especially the fast-moving dialogue. But she can't be regarded as a serious novelist, and the characters are very pasteboard—the same ones used over and over again, really.

And so much of her is uneven. Well, I suppose that is inevitable with a huge output spanning so many years. She died a very old lady. It's only fair to judge her by her best, not the worst of her work, and the best is remarkably ingenious. It's all very neat; it's all very clever, but I don't think we were trying to do the same things.

SELECTED SECONDARY BIBLIOGRAPHY

Benstock, Bernard. "The Clinical World of P. D. James," in *Twentieth-Century Women Novelists*, edited by Thomas F. Staley. Totowa, NJ: Barnes & Noble, 1982, cloth, p. 104-129.

Budd, Elaine. "P. D. James: Ordinary Lives, Extraordinary Deaths," in *13 Mistresses of Murder*. New York: Frederick Ungar Publishing Co., 1986, cloth, p. 65-74.

Cooper-Clark, Diana. "Interview with P. D. James," in *Designs of Darkness: Interviews with Detective Novelists*. Bowling Green, OH: Bowling Green State University Popular Press, 1983, cloth, p. 15-32.

Gidez, Richard B. *P. D. James*. Boston: Twayne Publishers, 1986, 153 p., cloth.

Harkness, Bruce. "P. D. James," in *Essays on Detective Fiction*, edited by Bernard Benstock. London: Macmillan, 1983, cloth, p. 119-141.

Heilbrun, Carolyn G. "James, P(hyllis) D(orothy)," in *Twentieth-Century Crime and Mystery Writers, Second Edition*, edited by John M. Reilly. New York: St. Martin's Press, 1985, cloth, p. 500-501.

Joyner, Nancy C. "P. D. James," in *10 Women of Mystery*. Bowling Green, OH: Bowling Green State University Popular Press, 1981, cloth, p. 108-123.

Siebenheller, Norma. *P. D. James*. New York: Frederick Ungar Publishing Co., 1981, x, 154 p., cloth.

H. R. F. Keating
(photo by Fay Godwin)

AN H. R. F. KEATING CHRONOLOGY

1926 Henry Reymond Fitzwalter Keating born October 31st at St. Leonards-on-Sea, Sussex, England.

1940 Attends Merchant Taylors' School at London (through 1944).

1945 Serves in the British Army (through 1948).

1948 Attends Trinity College, Dublin.

1952 Receives his B.A. from Trinity College (Vice-Chancellor's Prose Prize).

1953 Marries Sheila Mary Mitchell. Works as Sub-Editor for the *Wiltshire Herald*, Swindon (through 1956).

1956 Appointed Sub-Editor for the *Daily Telegraph*, London (through 1958).

1958 Works as Sub-Editor for *The Times*, London (through 1960).

1959 First mystery, *Death and the Visiting Firemen* published by Victor Gollancz (U.S. edition, 1973).

1960 Second book, *Zen There Was Murder*, published.

1961 *A Rush on the Ultimate* (U.S. edition, 1982).

1962 *The Dog It Was That Died* released.

1963 Moves to William Collins with *Death of a Fat God* (U.S. edition, 1966). Collins remains his publisher to date.

1964 *The Perfect Murder* published (U.S. edition, 1965). Receives Crime Writers Association Golden Dagger Award.

1965 *Is Skin-Deep, Is Fatal.* Receives Edgar Award from Mystery Writers of America.

1966 *Inspector Ghote's Good Crusade.*

1967 *Inspector Ghote Caught in Meshes* (U.S. edition, 1968). Appointed Crime Books Reviewer for *The Times* (through 1983).

1968 *Inspector Ghote Hunts the Peacock.*

1969 *Inspector Ghote Plays a Joker.* Co-authors *Understanding Pierre Teilhard de Chardin* with Maurice Keating (Lutterworth Press).

1970 *Inspector Ghote Breaks an Egg* (U.S. edition, 1971). Serves as Chairman of the Crime Writers Association (through 1971). Wins an award from *Ellery Queen's Mystery Magazine.*

1971 *Inspector Ghote Goes by Train* (U.S. edition, 1972). Also published this year is Keating's first mainstream novel, *The Strong Man* (Heinemann). Writes first radio play, an adaptation of *The Dog It Was That Died.*

1972 *Inspector Ghote Trusts the Heart* (U.S. edition, 1973). Also edits *Blood on the Mind* for Macmillan.

1974 *Bats Fly Up for Inspector Ghote.* Also publishes second mainstream novel, *The Underside.*

1975 *A Remarkable Case of Burglary* (U.S. edition, 1976). Also publishes the nonfiction work, *Murder Must Appetize* (Lemon Tree Press).

1976 *Filmi, Filmi, Inspector Ghote* (U.S. edition, 1977).

1977 Edits *Agatha Christie: First Lady of Crime* (Weidenfeld & Nicolson).

1978 Edits *Crime Writers: Reflections on Crime Fiction* (BBC Publications).

1979 *Inspector Ghote Draws a Line.* Also publishes the nonfiction work, *Sherlock Holmes: The Man and His World* (Thames and Hudson).

1980 Wins an Edgar Award from MWA. Publishes *The Murder of the Maharajah.*

1981 *Go West, Inspector Ghote.* Receives a Gold Dagger Award from the Crime Writers Association.

1982 Edits *Whodunit? A Guide to Crime, Suspense, and Spy Fiction*, and also publishes a novel, *The Lucky Alphonse*, and a nonfiction work, *Great Crimes.*

1984 *The Sheriff of Bombay.*

1985 *Mrs. Craggs: Crimes Cleaned Up.*

1986 *Under a Monsoon Cloud.* Also publishes the nonfiction work, *Writing Crime Fiction.*

1987 *The Body in the Billiard Room* and *Crime & Mystery: The 100 Best Books.*

1988 *Dead on Time.*

1989 *Inspector Ghote, His Life and Crimes* (collection) and *The Bedside Companion to Crime.*

1990 *The Iciest Sin.*

III.
AN INTERVIEW WITH
H. R. F. KEATING

SALWAK: How do you account for your interest in crime fiction?

KEATING: I suppose from reading it, not at my father's knee, but at my mother's knee. She was a great reader of detective stories, and she weaned me onto them, I suppose when I was about eleven or twelve, and I read them avidly. I think even then I must have had some notion that one day I would write. I can remember taking some sort of solemn oath to myself that I would never *not* write a detective story, with a murderer to be discovered. In those days, you know, I was a great guesser. I would say to my mother, "I know," and she would say, "I know, too." And so I took this oath that I would never write one that wasn't a pure detective story. And alas, I've broken it time and again since.

SALWAK: Who were some of the writers you read as a child?

KEATING: Dorothy Sayers. Agatha Christie, rather less, I think. We liked the ones with the backgrounds—Gladys Mitchell, E. R. Punshon (there's a name from the past). His weren't very good, but we enjoyed them. Latterly there's Michael Innes, but I suppose that was when I was teenaged and still able to appreciate him.

SALWAK: Did any of these writers influence your own writing?

KEATING: No, I don't feel that anybody has had a direct influence on my writing, but I did feel, for a long time, an obligation to have a proper puzzle plot. I obviously owe that to all the people (indiscriminately) who wrote puzzle stories in the past. It's only really very recently that I've come to see that you can write a mystery without really challenging the reader in the way that it used to be done. And that that's enough: merely propounding the mystery and in due course producing an answer, without detailed and meticulous clueing. That makes a very good book.

SALWAK: But what intrigues the reader of your books, I feel, goes beyond the actual puzzle. You have great characters, too.

KEATING: Oh yes. I mean, I couldn't write pure puzzle fiction. I'd certainly want to have people who are reasonably like people in life. I've gone further, in fact, because the first one I did, the first one published, *Death and the Visiting Firemen,* was a fairly straightforward detective story, with an interesting background and also, I think, quite good characters—although I did not go terribly deeply into them. But then when I'd done that I suddenly saw that you could do more with the detective story. That you could use it really just as you use a novel to make a point about something in life that you believed. And the thing that I believed in, one of the things that bugged me the most, was the subject of telling lies, which is fine for a detective story. And that was how I came to write my second, *Zen There Was Murder,* which is really more about telling lies then about Zen.

SALWAK: How did that interest come about?

KEATING: I can remember the traumatic moment in my early life when I realized that lies were more complicated than I'd been told. As a small boy I'd learnt: you mustn't tell lies. And that was that. But one day I was out with my father—I must have been about nine, I suppose—in a car, and an uncle was in the front with him and I was crouched in the back. My father shot a red light, and there was a policeman on the far side. The policeman pulled him up and said, "You'll have to be summoned." And that was that. I knew my father had been talking to my uncle and had just not seen the red light. We went home, and we had tea outside under the big cherry tree that we had. It was early summer. And my mother was there, and my father started to recount this incident. And somehow it wasn't his fault at all. It was the policeman's fault. And then I realized that grownups told lies, my *father* told lies, and this must have been really quite a turning point in my life.

So ever since I've been bugged by, "How wrong *was* it to tell lies?" When writing the second book, I thought I could say something about telling lies. At that time, too, Zen Buddhism was a fad over here, and so, for the background of the book, I took Zen, which does reflect very much on lies. I found that I could say things about lies by giving each of the characters a different viewpoint on telling lies—ranging from one of those people who absolutely objects to lying in any way to the sort of pathological liar. And I made the whole book turn on that.

SALWAK: "Oh what a tangled web we weave, when first we practice to deceive"—that's a predominant feature of your work, isn't it? What other themes are important to you as a writer?

KEATING: There have been other considerations in the other books. *A Rush on the Ultimate*—that was violence. I don't know quite what came first there: perhaps the notion of writing about croquet, because originally the book was to be called *With Mallet Aforethought*, a play on the legal term "With Malice Aforethought." And this arose (a terrible pun) when I was doing some repairs to the house using a wooden mallet, and suddenly the phrase jumped into my mind, and I wondered if I could write a crime story based on do-it-yourself repairs to the house—I hate doing them—and then decided, "no I couldn't." But then I thought of the other sort of mallet, the croquet mallet, and I thought, "yes, croquet!"

It so happened that an old friend of my mother was one-time champion of England at croquet, and has written the standard work on the subject. So I asked him if he'd tell me all about croquet. He took me out to Hurlingham where they were playing, two rather elderly gentlemen in mild rain fighting out a round in the All-England Championship, watched just by me, raincoat-less. But I must have asked myself: all right, if I'm going to use croquet as a background, and obviously have some murder puzzle, what does croquet *say* to me?

Paradoxically, what it said to me, because it's such a pleasant sport on the surface, was, "violence." And violence was one of those things that again bugged me—is it ever right to be violent? Of course, it must be. There are certain situations when you have to use violence. And so the range of characters in that book goes from the very mildest to someone who has escaped from Broadmoor Asylum because of his uncheckable violence. The book is full of reflections on violence, but I hope concealed. I mean, I didn't ever want to make it overt. I wanted the reader at the end to find himself or herself thinking about violence to some extent but not saying, "Oh, yeah, I must underline that passage." I think that's the way the crime novel can work, to some extent, better than the novel proper. You can say things, and you perhaps say them more efficiently because they're concealed in this sweet package.

SALWAK: Then you do see yourself as a moralist?

KEATING: Oh, yes, "H. R. F. Keating: Crime Writer as Moralist." It's the nature of the beast. Some of us are born with more active consciences than others. I've worried about things ever since I can remember. Am I doing right? In some ways it's good, but in other ways it hampers you from doing things; however, that's the way one is, and it comes out in the writing.

SALWAK: I can certainly see it in the character of Inspector Ghote, an humanitarian in conflict with society, a man generally disappointed with the people around him.

KEATING: I was interviewed once by the *Radio Times*, and the heading they put on it was "Inspector Ghote, *c'est moi*." Very true. I mean, he *is* me. All right, he's Indian and he's a slight figure physically, though tough enough, and I'm not, I'm British and we're miles apart in many ways. But inside him is a lot of me.

SALWAK: And the reader relates to him, feels sympathy for him, in spite of Ghote's failings?

KEATING: Yes. At least I hope that he is sympathetic (particularly if he's like me). It's tricky. If you give a man a lot of failings and he's still got to triumph every time, it's a narrow tightrope you walk. Writing about him for the second and third time, I had not so much to alter his character as to bring out aspects of it, perhaps my character, that weren't as noticeable in the first book. I had to give him a certain sort of shrewdness and physical toughness, for one thing. That physical toughness I haven't got. I made him a very persistent runner in one of the books, so that he does have some heroic qualities. Otherwise, it's very very difficult to write about someone who is constantly making mistakes, constantly getting everything wrong, and who is, in any case, not very lifelike.

SALWAK: How was Inspector Ghote created? He must have been solidly in your mind before you began your first novel.

KEATING: No, curiously enough: I think he happened by accident, in a flash of intuition. I was actually very lucky. You can say, "Oh, I want to write a new detective story, and I must have a hero and what he should be like. Well, there have been this sort and this sort. Perhaps he should be this, and he would need to have this quality and this." But I don't think those kinds of books are ultimately very successful, with their artificially constructed heroes. What happened to me (I tell the story and I don't know how much I've made it true by repeated telling) is that I was reading a geography book about India. This was when I was preparing to write about India. And I suddenly looked up and I thought, he'll be that sort of a man. So in a way he came to me in a flash, basically as is. I suppose I saw a *naïve*, Candide-like person. Because of his *naïveté* he would see things with a clear eye, almost like a child. So he came to me all at once. He came to me from myself. I'm a reasonably sophisticated person. I've been a journalist and all that. But I do have a *naïve* side to my character or perhaps a *naïve* center. I'm apt to believe what people tell me, and apt to see things in a quite simple way. Which I think is good. I mean, the *enfant terrible* sees that the emperor has no clothes. So Ghote came to me really out of intuition. And I've been able to switch him in various directions and to broaden his character since.

SALWAK: Why India? I believe that it was ten years later before you actually visited the country. Why not write about England, which you knew?

KEATING: Oh well, there's a terribly commercial reason for that. I was writing these early ones, like *A Rush on the Ultimate,* set in what we call in England the prep school—a private school for boys between the ages of seven and thirteen. My father was headmaster of one, and this was a background I knew. I combined it with croquet. And American publishers said it was too British for them, as I can well see. I sometimes say rather snidely that American publishers are only interested in houses with libraries and with bodies in that library, but that's not really true. But they quite rightly only wanted to publish books with backgrounds that, perhaps with a small jump, their readers could relate to. And mine were really too English and too small-scale for that. So I wasn't being published in America. My agent said, "They say you're too English." So I thought, what can I do to avoid this? India must have been in the air in 1963, I suppose. I don't know why. The Beatles went there, but I think that was a bit later. The hippies were going there, and then there was a lot of talk in international politics about a third force, and you thought here perhaps was hope for the world in the cold war days. Nehru and Tito could lead us out of the impasse. And so for various reasons, India was in the air.

Then one evening I was going to a party and someone came here to give me a lift. I was asking them about themselves, and they said, "Well, I'm just back from India." And I said, "Oh, I was thinking of setting a crime story in India." This was a very enthusiastic character, and he said, "Any help I can give you, it's a marvelous idea." And really on the strength of that I thought, "Okay, I'll do it."

But in another piece of luck—luck's very important to a writer—I seem to have an affinity with the Indian mind. I mean, Indians more than once have remarked on this. I suppose I could have chosen a country which wasn't sympathetic to me, and I knew really very little about India. I was going to call him Inspector Ghosh, because I thought that gave a sort of wide-eyed feel, to me as an Englishman. To Indians, however, "Ghosh" is a Bengali name, and I had decided that I ought to set my books in Bombay, because it was the most Westernized city in India. There would be a lot of things that I would know about. But using a character called Ghosh there would be the equivalent of calling a French detective Ivan Ivanovich.

My acquaintance from India, when I showed him a sort of synopsis, suggested "Ghote" as a substitute. In some ways this was very good. Ghote is a Marathi name—Bombay is in the state of Maharahstra—but actually fairly rare as a surname. So I didn't get into libel troubles. The police in India tend to run in families. Had I chosen one of those names I could have well found myself saddled with a real Inspector Sawant, or whatever. It ultimately would have caused trouble. On the other hand, a lot of people don't know how to pronounce "Ghote." You sound the final "e," you know, and, if you want to be very correct, you aspirate the initial "G." But what do I do when people come up to me and say, "I love your Inspector *Goat*"? I never know whether to correct them or say, "How nice."

SALWAK: Would it be fair to say that you also have an element of travelogue in your novels?

KEATING: Right from a child I liked the background setting in detective stories, whether it was Dorothy L. Sayers's advertising agency or whatever. It was something that you didn't know about and you learned painlessly about. India obviously provided just that sort of background. In fact, in my early books—there are four of them—I avoided using a police detective in England, because somewhere I had read that you can easily make mistakes in using a police official in a British setting, with readers by the hundreds writing in and pointing them out. So I thought, well, I won't have a regular detective, but to maintain a certain continuity I'll use a different, rather extraordinary background for each book. The first one had a coach-and-four taking a party of American businessmen—they are fire assessors—up to London from Southhampton, because I'd been on such a coach and I thought that's a curious background. Then Zen Buddhism was another curious background. And croquet another. I saw myself sort of constantly producing books with new and interesting settings. India was really just another such backdrop on a rather larger scale than the others.

SALWAK: *Is Skin-Deep, Is Fatal* is the odd one out, isn't it? Was it written before your earliest novels?

KEATING: It comes out of series, really. I'd written *The Perfect Murder,* the first Ghote story, and it had been published and got good reviews, but hadn't at that time yet won the Gold Dagger from the Crime Writers. My publisher said to me that he didn't think that India was a subject which people would go on liking, I think with some justification. I can remember my wife telling a friend that I wrote books about India, and she said, "Oh, not all those *charpoys.*" I thought perhaps it was all a bit much, the Indian background. At that time, in my moralistic way, I wanted to write something about beauty contests and the nonsense that they were, and so I wrote this book, *Is Skin-Deep, Is Fatal*, set in Soho at a pageant.

But then *The Perfect Murder* won its prize and it was obvious that the thing to do was to go on with Inspector Ghote. Indeed, I'd gone down to interview Marjorie Allingham, who was another of my heroes as a boy, and she said to me, "It's a good thing to have a running hero because half your readers like the hero and half of them like you, and you double your stakes." And so Ghote lived on, although he was really only intended to be the hero of one book. Again, I was lucky there, partly because he is me, and I've been happy to write about him again and again. He's never grown stale on me.

SALWAK: What makes for good detective fiction?

KEATING: Fundamentally, you've got to have an intriguing puzzle. It's a nuisance in a way, since I'm often more interested in what I've got to say. And then you need to have something memorable. It can be the puzzle or the background, if it's slightly unusual (but not too). It's easy to say, "Oh, I must find some very unusual setting," and you'll find something so exotic that nobody's really interested in it. So you've got to find something in between.

The other thing, of course, is your character, whether it's the villain or the murdered person. I'm assuming that you're using a series detective, so for the really exotic you need someone else, a character who just stands out. You have to tell a good story without ever deviating for a moment, and it should be something you're passionate about, maybe even the puzzle aspect. It's the passion that soaks into the pages that makes a really first-class crime novel.

SALWAK: In *Murder Must Appetize* you discuss what you find most appealing about the detective fiction of the 1930s.

KEATING: Those writers enjoyed so much describing their fierce little military chief constables and associates, and their vague vicars; and yes, even their outrageous meals and afternoon teas. I, too, enjoy calling to my mind's eye exotic scenes in India and the equally exotic people. It doesn't always work, but when I get hold of an interesting character, I'm delighted when he comes back onto the pages again and behaves in his characteristic way.

SALWAK: In his book *Bloody Murder*, Julian Symons refers to your early novels as "semi-surrealist."

KEATING: I took that as praise, and I was very pleased. He refers specifically to my third novel, in which I included descriptions that read almost like a film scenario: "Dawn. Pale light creeping over the water. Silhouette." I wrote the whole of the book—*A Rush on the Ultimate*—in this style, basically leaving out the verbs, which gave it the semi-surrealist tone which so pleased Julian Symons, a tone that I kept up for two or three books more.

SALWAK: Could you tell me something about your writing methods?

KEATING: Well, I write in short bursts at high speed, on the typewriter as fast as I can clatter. I think if you're doing it very fast it opens a passage to the back of the brain, if you like, to intuition. You find you've put down, or thought of, a word and you say to yourself, "That's nonsense." But then you pause for a moment and you think, "No, it's exactly the right word." So when I'm actually writing I'll sit at the typewriter for twenty minutes, even half an hour, going full steam ahead. I'll sometimes leave a gap when I can't think of the exact word. And then I get a sort of fuzzy feeling and the concentration is gone. I stop. Then I go back to the story again for a short time. I'll read what I wrote last thing at night. This is a tip I got from Graham Greene in *A Sort of Life*. He says he always reads what he's written last thing at night, to send it down to what he calls the *nègre*, the ghost figure that works for you, the zombie. And then in the morning I read it over again and correct, and when the whole thing is finished, I revise quite heavily. I write from the beginning to the end. I couldn't be one of these people who writes the scene that they think of and then patches it in.

SALWAK: Do you do a lot of pre-writing?

KEATING: I like to think that the idea for a book must come a couple of years before I actually get down to it, so that something probably has been going on in the back of the head, and it gradually becomes a tough idea. Then I begin by asking, "What is this book to be about?" Someone once said that you ought to be able to say in one sentence what a novel is about. I like to hit on that sentence. I like, if possible, to hit on the title, too, because it tells you what it's about. Sometimes I haven't been able to, and as the book's grown I say I must have a title and there's twenty or thirty possible ones written out on a sheet of paper.

From there, of course, it must be a murder story and it must usually be a puzzle story; certainly in the early days it was. I do have pages of a notebook for each character, with a few things jotted down about them, generally their age, if I remember to do it. And I like to hit on the one thing about them that is most characteristic. It may be a big nose or it may be the sort of clothes they wear or even something that they do. So at each time I think of the character I hold that in my mind and it reminds me what I should be writing about.

SALWAK: What tends to spark your imagination?

KEATING: Most of the times it's theme. I'll be walking along and see somebody doing something and think, "Oh, that's very typical of that sort of person." Or it may be something I read in the paper. I think, "Oh, that's a fascinating idea." Just before going to give a talk somewhere about being a writer, I was waiting to go in, and I was flipping through the paper. I saw a little bit about one of those jungle children that had been found, a wild boy, and I thought, "This is fascinating—the human being grown up without any preconceptions." And I thought, "One day I will try and work that into a Ghote book."

Another thing from the paper was three lines saying that in Japan a millionaire's son had not been kidnapped, but his chauffeur's son had been. This struck me as being poignant and fascinating straightaway, and I thought, "Oh, well, I can easily transfer that to India and maybe change the driver or something." It was only later that I wondered why I found the story so affecting. It really asks how much you should trust the heart, and indeed I called the book *Inspector Ghote Trusts the Heart*. So it's generally the theme that comes first, but sometimes something out of the blue strikes me as fascinating, and I realize that it does go back to some obsession I have.

SALWAK: How personal is your work?

KEATING: Very. That's why when you asked me who do I feel has influenced me the most, I answered: "I don't feel that anybody has influenced me in quite that way," other than the marvelous examples of other writers being published, which tends to encourage you. All writing is personal, and you shouldn't allow yourself to be heavily influenced by anyone.

SALWAK: Many of your novels feature unique variations on the traditional elements of detective fiction. You have a passenger train mystery, for example, and a version of the locked room mystery in *Go West, Inspector Ghote*. Are there any traditions you haven't tapped but would like to?

KEATING: Not specifically. In *Go West* I wanted to write about materialism and mysticism, though in fact that book derived from someone saying to me that I ought to take Inspector Ghote to America. When I thought of what in America would interest me, it was the odd combination of materialism and mysticism. I was able to switch them in an interesting way, so that California represents the mystic element and India the materialist. Having thought there would have to be some mystic manifestation like the translocation of a body, I then found that this led into the locked-room idea. I have read a great many crime stories over the years, and have reviewed hundreds for *The Times*, so I have seen just about every variation of the theme. And if some future book naturally leads me to another one of these classic situations, I don't think I should be able to resist it.

SALWAK: Did your novel writing benefit from your book reviewing experience?

KEATING: A little, I suppose, in that the process of analyzing these novels forced me to think about the nature of the crime story. I've got a notebook of such observations, and have put some of them together in *Whodunit?* and other works. Somewhere I once read a comment that the crime story is essentially a fairy story in which good triumphs over evil. I certainly had this very much in mind while writing *Go West, Inspector Ghote,* and even used some fantasy imagery in it. Ghote sees the people he comes up against as giants or ogres, and the structure of the story is basically an heroic quest. Ghote must travel to this mysterious place, California, which he has only heard about.

I was a bit worried when I first began reviewing crime stories that I would find other people's styles rubbing off in my own works, or that I would unconsciously borrow plot elements from unrelated works. But no, I find you can switch your mind from being one sort of person to another, and Keating-as-reviewer doesn't really connect with Keating-as-writer.

SALWAK: *The Lucky Alphonse* represents a departure for you.

KEATING: Not really: I've written three mainstream novels, and this is the fourth. It's a slightly experimental and unusual one, if you like. I was thinking—indeed, had been thinking for years—about music, and the symphony, and what it is that links together the movements of a symphony. Why do three quite different movements make up one work? I wondered if I could not do something rather similar with the novel. So this is a story consisting of three novellas. The hero in each one has a similar name, a version of Alphonse. The title derives from a classic dirty joke.

The first tale is about a young Indian diplomat from Goa, which is how he comes to be called Afonso. The second tells the tale of a petty Irish crook called Fonsy, and the third deals with a German history lecturer called Alfons. In each section their situation is the same: they're caught in the middle between two forces. This is another of my obsessions. I believe that that's the best place to be, to find the middle path between any two extremes.

In the first story the diplomat is caught between two women he loves equally, who represent different things. There is the earth-mother Indian he's married to, and there's the American girl in UNESCO, who is very intelligent. He falls in love with her, but he continues with both. In the end he perhaps commits suicide, perhaps dies accidentally in a car crash, because it's just too much, these two forces. Then you're in Ireland with a petty crook who makes a living partly by helping gangs, partly by informing to the police. He is caught between the gang leader and the police boss. More by luck than anything else he manages to squeeze through and land reasonably safe in the end, protected from both of them. In the third part the German history lecturer is called to a little country between South Africa—slightly disguised South Africa—and a slightly disguised Communist power to the north, and this little country is caught between these two forces. He's asked by his ex-pupil, the prince of the country and prime minister, to advise him, and they do eventually triumph and manage to preserve the integrity of the country.

I hope that when the reader has read all three stories he will have a feeling for being in the middle of things, perhaps stronger than if he had read just one novel with, say, a hero in that situation.

SALWAK: Your book on *Sherlock Holmes* must have been enjoyable to research.

KEATING: I was asked to do it by the publisher. The nicest thing of all was that it meant that I had to read and re-read those magnificent stories. He's a great example of the intuitive, Conan Doyle. In California I saw one of his manuscripts, and it's dashed off. He got right back to the intuition at the back of the brain, and that's why they last so well, I think. I found that in reading those stories and examining the history of the time, the one reflected very much on the other, which I hadn't necessarily expected. I found it very interesting that Holmes was typically a man of his time and that equally the events of the time reflect on him. Doing some of the research for the illustrations was fascinating, too: going through the files of the *Illustrated London News* and finding things that were absolutely applicable to the stories.

SALWAK: *The Sheriff of Bombay* differs from your other Ghote novels quite markedly.

KEATING: I finally tackled sex, which I've never really approached in the crime story before. I think someone of my generation still finds it pretty difficult to write about the subject. So although in that book I don't have Ghote falling desperately in love or anything like that, he does get involved in the sex world of Bombay. He is deputed to take an aging British film star around to what they called the cages—the red light area. They're not really cages, but they have barred doors behind which the girls display themselves.

They're one of the sights of Bombay, to which I was taken on my second visit to India. The police inspectors were very proud to show me the seamier sides of the city. I was able to use a lot of the information I gained in one or two evening outings in *Sheriff*.

SALWAK: And so Ghote gets involved in the world of prostitutes?

KEATING: Various prostitutes tell him their stories, portions of which I culled from a book of interviews with prostitutes in very vivid Indian English. In this way I was able to look at the complications of sex—how one action can mean one thing to one person and almost exactly the opposite to another. This is an ideal situation for a crime story. So I was pretty pleased with myself.

SALWAK: How do your most recent Ghote mysteries compare with the earlier ones?

KEATING: I think that they've advanced in many ways—at least I hope so! They're slightly more serious, and I've been able to go into character a little more deeply. I certainly have found that my knowledge of India has grown in the interim. Whereas in the early books I had to use every fact I could scrape together, I now find—having more or less continuously read about India, watched TV about India, even been to India—that I've really stored up a lot of information about the country and its people, and I can now sort of select the best fact out of three for any particular situation. So I feel that the new books are a good deal more authentic than the very early ones were. And a little deeper, too.

SALWAK: What brought about this change?

KEATING: In a way I was challenged by Len Deighton. When I sent him *The Sheriff of Bombay*, he wrote back that he liked it very much, but felt I could go deeper into characterization. He felt that I always wrote at a little distance. And indeed I did. I thought I would try to write something closer, more emotional perhaps. And so I devised a situation for Ghote where he was hard-pressed in every possible way, and put myself in his shoes and and saw what happened.

SALWAK: This led to *Under a Monsoon Cloud*. Is the central plot derived from real experiences?

KEATING: When I was in India I talked to a senior Indian policeman. He told me a story about a very high-flying policeman who had been in charge of a police station and had accidentally killed one of his subordinates. They had covered up the crime by pretending he'd drowned in the sea. This official I was talking to had actually been the one dispatched to investigate the "accident." Later the whole truth came out and the man responsible, who had a good career in front of him, committed suicide.

I've been rather hesitant about describing this because I use practically the same story line, and I now can't remember which was the original and which was my elaboration. Anyhow, in *Under a Monsoon Cloud* Ghote assists a high-ranking police officer in covering an accidental killing of a stupid subordinate, and then it all begins to unravel. The high-ranking police officer commits suicide and Ghote is brought up before a disciplinary board. He is now in the position of having to decide whether he will try and brazen it out or admit what happened, thereby giving up his career in the police force.

Since Ghote thinks that being a detective is the only thing that he can do in life, tremendous pressures of every sort begin building. So this book represents a much more serious examination of Ghote's character, and it does come off, I think (one never knows with one's own books). In re-reading it I got the feeling that much of it could not have been construed in any other way. That's always a good feeling.

SALWAK: How did you decide on the title?

KEATING: I've decided not to put Inspector Ghote in the titles anymore, which gives me (once again) a certain amount of room to maneuver. The whole thing is set in two monsoon seasons: in one monsoon where the accidental killing takes place, and where Ghote and this senior officer take the corpse through pouring rain out into a lake and sink it; and then the trial occurs in the following monsoon.

SALWAK: I believe you've started a second series of crime novels.

KEATING: I wanted to see if I could write books that would reach a wider audience—chiefly the American paperback audience, which the Ghote books don't do. There's interest in America in India, but it's by and large confined to a top layer of intelligent readers. Your ordinary paperback buyer isn't really interested in an Indian detective—or at least he hasn't been up to now. So my agent suggested that I write a series of books that would appeal to that sort of audience. I devised the notion of a Victorian governess who gets involved in crimes. In the first book, *The Governess*, she herself is accused of the murder of the head of the household—*pater familias*, the old Victorian bit. And she has to fight for her own life.

And then in the next one—*The Man of Gold*—she's moved on to a different household ruled over by a tremendous Victorian miser who eventually is murdered, of course. His son has begun to fall in love with Miss Unwin, my governess, and he is taken to the police station for questioning. She is determined to find who the real culprit is, and so prove to the police that this man who loves her couldn't have committed the murder. But of course I had to arrange things so that they don't get married happily ever after; otherwise, she would cease to be a governess.

SALWAK: I suppose a Victorian governess would make quite a good detective—knowing children, and understanding as much psychology as was known in those days.

KEATING: But what you don't think of when you begin is how to create a scenario where she can move from year to year into different families, with each one of them experiencing a murder as she arrives. So for the third one—*Into the Valley of Death*, which harks back to the Crimean War—I contrived a maid who will assist Miss Unwin. She is a very rough and ready servant who generally works in the same house as the governess and acts as her Watson. And this time she's summoned by this girl who's gone to work down in the country. So the situation isn't quite the same. She isn't actually the governess. She just comes to the nearby pub where the landlord has been accused of murder and is about to be hanged in a week. And Miss Unwin has a week to find—and of course does discover—the identity of the real murderer.

SALWAK: Have you ever employed supernatural elements, much as Henry James does in "The Turn of the Screw"?

KEATING: I don't like the notion of the supernatural in that way. Crime stories should be a matter of rational thought. Having said that, I would like to write about people like William Douglas Hume, the spiritualist and subject of Browning's poem. It's possible that I could involve Miss Unwin in that sort of setting, but I wouldn't want to have the supernatural involved. Much more the psychic, if you can see the distinction. No ghosts, but communication with the dead—which is a different thing—or the belief that you are communicating with the dead, thought transference, or similar subjects.

SALWAK: Why use the penname, Evelyn Harvey, for this new series?

KEATING: I thought that as I had a female heroine, I would choose a forename that could be either man or woman. Hence Evelyn. And then I picked the surname from an old family name. My father was named John Hervui: it's distant, and extremely aristocratic, deriving from the dukes of Bristol, the ones who went around Europe founding all those Bristol Hotels. Perhaps Inspector Ghote would approve!

SELECTED SECONDARY BIBLIOGRAPHY

Hill, Reginald. "Keating, H(enry) R(eymond) F(itzwalter)," in *Twentieth-Century Crime and Mystery Writers*, edited by John M. Reilly. New York: St. Martin's Press, 1985, cloth, p. 518-520.

Keating, H. R. F. "Publisher's Note: The One-Hundred-and-First Choice," in *Crime and Mystery: The 100 Best Books*. New York: Carroll & Graf, 1987, cloth, p. 211-212.

A RUTH RENDELL CHRONOLOGY

1930 Born February 17th in London.

1948 Works as a reporter and Sub-Editor for the *Express* and *Independent* newspapers, West Essex (through 1952).

1950 Marries Donald Rendell (divorced).

1964 First book, *From Doon with Death*, published in England by Hutchinson (U.S. edition, 1965).

1965 Publishes *To Fear a Painted Devil* and *Vanity Dies Hard* from John Long.

1966 *Vanity Dies Hard* published in the U.S. by Doubleday as *In Sickness and in Health*.

1967 New books include *A New Lease of Death* (published in the U.S. in 1970 as *Sins of the Fathers*) and *Wolf to the Slaughter* (U.S. edition, 1968).

1968 *The Secret House of Death* (U.S. edition, 1969).

1969 *The Best Man to Die* (U.S. edition, 1970).

1970 Publishes *A Guilty Thing Surprised*.

1971 *No More Dying Then* (U.S. edition, 1972) and *One Across, Two Down*.

1972 *Murder Being Once Done*.

1973 *Some Lie and Some Die*.

1974 *The Face of Trespass.*

1975 Wins an Edgar Award from Mystery Writers of America. Publishes *Shake Hands Forever.*

1976 Wins a Crime Writers Association Golden Dagger Award. Publishes *A Demon in My View* (U.S. Edition, 1977) and *The Fallen Curtain and Other Stories (of Suspense).*

1977 Wins a second Golden Dagger. Publishes *A Judgement in Stone* (U.S. edition, 1978).

1978 *A Sleeping Life.*

1979 *Make Death Love Me* and *Means of Evil and Other Stories.*

1980 *The Lake of Darkness.*

1981 *Put on by Cunning* (published in the U.S. as *Death Notes*).

1982 *Master of the Moor.*

1983 *Speaker of Mandarin.*

1984 *The Tree of Hands* and *The Killing Doll.*

1985 *An Unkindness of Ravens* and *The New Girl Friend and Other Stories.*

1986 Publishes *Live Flesh, Heartstones,* and the first mystery under the penname Barbara Vine: *A Dark-Adapted Eye.*

1987 *Talking to Strange Men, A Warning to the Curious, Collected Short Stories,* and *A Fatal Inversion* (as Barbara Vine). Also edits M. R. James' *A Warning to the Curious* (a collection of his short stories).

1988 *The Veiled One* and *The House of Stairs* (as Barbara Vine).

1989 *The Bridesmaid, Ruth Rendell's Suffolk* (nonfiction), and *Undermining the Central Line* (nonfiction; with Colin Ward).

1990 *Going Wrong* and *Gallowglass* (as Barbara Vine). Edits *Unguarded Hours*.

1991 *The Copper Peacock, and Other Stories*.

Ruth Rendell

IV.
AN INTERVIEW WITH RUTH RENDELL

SALWAK: Have you always wanted to be a writer?

RENDELL: I don't know so much about "being a writer," but I always wanted to write. Until my first book was published I didn't really believe I would ever "be a writer" in the sense of someone whose work is published and avidly read and even acclaimed.

SALWAK: Did the fact that you were an only child have any bearing on your development as a writer?

RENDELL: This sort of question is very hard to answer. How do I know? I am only one person. In order to tell I should have had to have grown up both with siblings as well as without them. My father and mother were both people with highly developed imaginations who read a lot. I might have reacted against this, but it so happens that I didn't.

SALWAK: How are your childhood experiences reflected in your fiction?

RENDELL: My parents were not happy together and quarrelled constantly in my presence. I realized from a very early age how clever, articulate people may hurt each other with words. In spite of this my parents were very close to their own families. My father, for example, adored his mother and his sisters. My mother regarded her sisters as her only friends. I think this has resulted in my filling my novels with blood relationships. I find it hard, for instance, to create a character without endowing him or her with a whole mass of relatives.

SALWAK: I read somewhere that your series character Wexford is partially derived from your father.

RENDELL: My son, who had been doing a psychology course at the time, asked me one day if I realized that Wexford was my father. I thought about that one, and replied that yes, he is—in part. My father was a teacher, not a policeman, and he was a lot more reticent and reserved than Wexford is, but he used to say Wexford-like things—or perhaps Wexford talks like my father. Wexford is also a lot like me.

SALWAK: How did the character develop?

RENDELL: He started off a lot tougher than he now is. When I realized he was going to be a popular series character that I was now stuck with, I started making him more sensitive and more cultivated. I now think he's gone a bit too far in that direction, and I shall have to pull him back.

SALWAK: Your early work as a reporter and sub-editor with the *Express* and *Independent* newspapers interests me.

RENDELL: Well, it doesn't interest *me*. I was a very bad journalist. I suppose all experience helps a novelist in some way, but I can't think of any specific help I got from working on what we called "the old *E* and *I*."

SALWAK: Why mystery and detective fiction?

RENDELL: I wrote my first one for fun, and it happened to be the only thing that I had then penned that a publishing house was actually willing to publish. Really! This is the cold truth! Later on I got fond of my Wexford and enjoyed figuring out the puzzle parts. Forensics really bore me. It is my psychological suspense novels that I like and enjoy writing best. To my mind the most wonderful thing that ever happened to the detective novel was when— sometime in the sixties, I suppose—it began to stop being just a crime story and started being a novel with police in it.

SALWAK: Since then, has there been a kind of constant learning process on your part, even though you are a master of your craft and have all these books behind you?

RENDELL: I have tried during the years since my first book was published to learn to write. I haven't bothered about learning about the police or weaponry or stuff like that, but I have tried to learn to write better. Now, I still don't write the way I should like to, but I think I make a better job of it than I once did.

SALWAK: What lessons did you learn from your editors?

RENDELL: My first editor (now, alas, dead) taught me to be a professional writer. From him I learned to sit down each day and write, to check and verify, to write economically and not at too great a length. He taught me the importance of delivering a manuscript when I said I would, reading proofs on time, and not to be slipshod; and when I had first achieved some success he kept me from becoming swollen-headed by praising me only sparingly and then with great restraint. His name was Gerald Austin and I shall mourn him always.

SALWAK: Your first published novel, *From Doon with Death*, appeared in 1964 when you were thirty-four. As a novelist relatively new to the world of detective fiction, what kinds of problems did you encounter?

RENDELL: I *ought* to have encountered the problem of not knowing anything about the police, but I simply shied away from it and when in doubt, left things out. I still know nothing about the police. Wexford isn't like a real policeman at all; I hope he is a bit like a *real* man. Of course real detectives in a real police force don't sit around and cudgel their brains as to what "eonism" means. They don't use their holidays to chase criminals about California. Wexford is a fantasy policeman in a fantasy world. The wonder is that thousands of readers (including policemen!) seem to like it this way.

SALWAK: Part of your appeal, I think, is that you are a master of the psychological thriller. Have you always had the capacity or the for frightening people?

RENDELL: I rather like being frightened myself—that is, frightened by fiction in one form or another. M. R. James can still terrify me, although I have read his stories over and over again. I know whole passages from them by heart. I never frighten myself. Before I ever had anything published I used to enjoy telling people stories—while camping, say, or around a fire on a winter's night—and watching them become pleasurably terrified. I have learnt to frighten readers by the excellent method of reading and studying writers greater than I, all of them masters in the art of inducing fear.

SALWAK: Is it easier to write about unhappy times, unhappy things, unhappy people?

RENDELL: Yes, it is easier, just as it is easier to create the bad rather than the good. I am moving towards creating happier people and those with at least a potential for goodness.

SALWAK: In *Vanity Dies Hard*, Alice thinks of "that dark side of her character, that pessimistic side that had always been liable to fear the worst." Is this true for most people? Is it true for yourself?

RENDELL: I really don't know if it is true for most people. A test, of course, is to ask people what "taking a risk" means to them. Mostly they answer that it means taking a chance of something bad resulting, though of course the implication is that it is just as likely to be something good. For my own part, I am not particularly pessimistic, tending to such attitudes as "most of what you are worried about has never happened," "life changes," "wait and see," and so on.

SALWAK: A lot of your characters seem filled with guilt.

RENDELL: My experience of life has taught me that most people feel pretty guilty a whole lot of the time. My generation and those before it were taught to feel guilty, and really I can't see that things have changed much. We are heirs of the Puritan conscience, aren't we? From the start we are told: "Don't you think you ought to visit grandma? Do you know how much you've hurt mummy?

That wasn't a very nice thing to say to Mrs. Crosthwaite. Did you write and thank Pat for your lovely present?" And so on.

SALWAK: What appeals to you about your fiction?

RENDELL: I write psychological suspense novels because in them I can say all the things I can't say in plain detective stories. Or at least that's part of why I write them.

SALWAK: Are most people capable of committing murder?

RENDELL: *I* am not capable of committing murder. I have given this some thought and cannot think of any situation in which I might commit murder, leaving out bashing someone in self-defense. Nor do I believe that most people are savages with just a thin veneer of civilization. Those I know well, my friends and relatives, seem to me to be on the whole gentle, cultivated people who are very kindly disposed towards humanity. On the other hand, I have encountered a lot of men and women I wouldn't be surprised to hear had murdered someone.

SALWAK: Is character a form of destiny?

RENDELL: Well, I shouldn't think so, Dr. Freud, would you? I mean, some of it may be inherited or inborn or however one puts it, but some of it—a whole lot—must come from environment, or else psychiatrists might just as well pack up their bags and go home. I don't think I know what destiny is. For instance, if the English murderer John Reginald Halliday Christie had encountered a loving, sympathetic woman when he was twenty or so, had married her and had two or three children, I should think the chances of his turning out to be a homicidal necrophiliac would have been considerably diminished. The destiny lobby would presumably say here that it wasn't in the cards for him to meet and marry such a woman, or that if he had she would soon have ceased to be loving and sympathetic. But who can tell? The only thing would be for God or whoever to create two of him and give them disparate roads to follow.

SALWAK: There's one passage in *Death Notes* that I'd like to use as a cue. Wexford says: "The complexity was in our own minds, Mike.

The case itself was simple and straightforward, and almost everything that took place was the result of accident or of chance."

RENDELL: Chance interests me. I like it much more than destiny. When out walking, I sometimes come to a possible choice of two ways and say to myself that if I take that other one my whole future life may be changed. It is something I enjoy speculating about.

SALWAK: The coincidence of the shared first initial and last name is important in *A Demon in My View*. How did that idea originate?

RENDELL: I was sharing a flat in a house in London with a cousin of mine. He has the rather common name of Richards. Another tenant in the house also was called Richards and they shared the first initial "M." Their mail got constantly mixed up. *Quod erat demonstrandum.*

SALWAK: Like many of your readers, I have also been struck by how much of your writing plays on linguistic clues. I can think of *Vanity Dies Hard* ("Saulsby"), *Death Notes* ("Fassbender"), and *A Sleeping Life* ("eonism"), and marvel at how honest you have been with the reader from the very beginning of these novels. You must have great fun with that approach.

RENDELL: The pleasure in writing such stories lies for me precisely in these linguistic games. I loved doing the "eonism" stuff. You would be amazed how scarcely anyone who read *A Sleeping Life* bothered to look the word up in a dictionary. A newspaper reviewer commented on this and admitted that he hadn't.

SALWAK: You're not at all explicit about sex in your novels, and yet it remains another recurring topic.

RENDELL: Well, I do think writers ought to be explicit about sex, absolutely explicit. I despise the attitude that says "it's not necessary" or "it's better to suggest than go into details." Although I don't care to have sex compared to eating, if you're going to describe a banquet in detail you equally ought to be able to describe the sex act as explicitly as is necessary for that particular story. There should be no holds barred. I am not a sexually inhibited person—except insofar as all of us are. I don't find it difficult or embarrassing to talk about sex, and I think I am as explicit about sex in my novels as I need to be, especially in *No More Dying Then*, *Wolf to the Slaughter*, *Make Death Love Me*, *The Lake of Darkness*, and *The Killing Doll*. Having said this, I would add that I find the emotions connected with sex and how people feel during the act of sex much more interesting than their physical movements. But surely most writers think like this, barring pornographers?

SALWAK: Have you an interest in the occult?

RENDELL: There is nothing occult in any of my novels, only the belief on the part of certain characters—Finn and his mother in *The Lake of Darkness*, Dolly in *The Killing Doll*—that the occult exists and is manifesting itself. I can't understand why readers have thought there were supernatural happenings in *The Killing Doll*. Surely it is apparent all this is going on only in Dolly's head.

SALWAK: You've expressed some unhappiness with your novel, *One Across, Two Down*?

RENDELL: Actually there are a number of my novels with which I'm dissatisfied, including *One Across, Two Down*, *Vanity Dies Hard*, *The Secret House of Death*, *Some Lie and Some Die*, and *Death Notes*, simply because I don't think they're very good. In fact, I regard them as my worst books, and if *Vanity Dies Hard* ranks at the very bottom, *One Across, Two Down* runs it a close second. Oh, it has an excellent plot and one or two good characters, but it's ruined by cliché-ridden, even slipshod writing. My aforementioned and ever-mourned editor, Gerald Austin (now editing celestial books, no doubt, works of dead genius tapping heavenly typewriters), said to me of it, "You've written *Payment Deferred* all over again, haven't you, Ruth?" Enough said.

SALWAK: You've had great success with Wexford. But are there any pitfalls in doing a series?

RENDELL: You can get a bit bored. And it's maddening when I've written what I think is a subtle and carefully worked out and psychologically sound thriller, only to be asked when the next Wexford is coming, because someone likes those best.

SALWAK: Is it easier to work with female or male characters?

RENDELL: I used to find men much easier, but now I'm doing women and getting better at it. I think this is as much because women are becoming people in this world as because I'm improving as a writer. The girl in my *Secret House of Death* is the last of the old-style heroines, the injured, abandoned little wife stoically taking in typing. Benet Archdale in *The Tree of Hands* is an untrammelled woman of the eighties, for whom it isn't necessary to keep messing about with clothes and hairstyles and finding herself a husband.

SALWAK: What sparks your imagination? An overheard conversation? A setting? An observed character?

RENDELL: All of those things, and little things that just happen. About ninety percent of the things that happen to Wexford in China during the plot of *Speaker of Mandarin* actually happened *to me* in China. When I noticed that in this part of the world (East Anglia) they put scarecrows in cherry trees to scare birds at harvest time, that gave me an idea for a short story ("The Orchard Walls"). Having a tree fall over in our wood and then having the top lopped off, and its root swung back into the crater, gave me another spark (for "Fen Hall").

SALWAK: What about England itself? Is Kingsmarkham a real place?

RENDELL: I've always lived in England, mostly in London, in many different parts of London, though as a child I also lived in different parts of the country, and now live in the country again. Kingsmarkham is very broadly based on a place called Midhurst in Sussex where I have not set foot since age nine, so it is a dream place based on a fantasy.

SALWAK: Do you keep a notebook? Do you have a daily routine?

RENDELL: I don't keep a notebook. I have an excellent memory for this sort of thing. I get lost all the time and can't find my way anywhere and forget people's names and even their faces, but I can remember everyone's phone numbers and, oddly enough, their birthdays. I mean, absurdly, they have only to tell me once. I remember ideas for plots quite well enough and jot odd things down on scraps of paper on my desk. They lie around for a week or two. I do have a routine. I sit down to work every morning at 9:30 and work till about 1:30, then maybe a bit more in the afternoons. It has become compulsive, ridiculous really. I am making a New Year resolution to be more flexible and get out of the way of thinking the heavens will fall if I actually set foot outside this room for half an hour one weekday morning.

SALWAK: Is there some kind of serendipity that comes from writing short stories that ultimately helps you do longer works?

RENDELL: I still write short stories to teach me to be economical, to be brief and succinct, and I think it's been quite a salutary discipline.

SALWAK: What are some of the rewards that come to the detective novelist?

RENDELL: Popularity and money! The drawbacks are legion. Idiots ask one how many people one has murdered this week. Fools ask my husband if he's not afraid to eat things I've cooked. Some old horror once asked me at a party if it was true I made my living by killing people. Of course there are other rewards. Let's rephrase your question and ask how it feels to write popular fiction. A great reward is charming letters from fans, people coming from long distances to hear one speak and bringing with them an old, half-forgotten paperback for one to inscribe. And I have lots of readers whose long illnesses have been made more bearable by reading my whole canon, and people who say that my books have helped them through depression, anxiety, or bereavement. Another nice thing has been winning my literary prizes, of which I am very proud.

SALWAK: Finally, what are the ingredients for a successful detective novel? What works for you?

RENDELL: Character, always character—for any novel. I maintain that if you don't care for the people, if you can't identify with them or feel empathy, you aren't going to care what happens. So you must have interesting original characters. An intellectual puzzle is what I like, but some writers go too far with this sort of thing, and become abstruse and precious. I like a tremendous climax, if I can do it, an amazing surprise, and then just before the end a mini-surprise with a twist. Not a *who*dunit necessarily (or even preferably), but certainly a *why*dunit or who-it-was-done-to—or something like that. In my Wexford books I usually write the whole book with one killer in mind, and then at the end change it to someone else. Of course this means re-writing the early chapters, but it does work. If I can deceive myself, you see, I can deceive even the sharpest of my readers!

SELECTED SECONDARY BIBLIOGRAPHY

Bakerman, Jane S. "Rendell, Ruth," in *Twentieth-Century Crime and Mystery Writers, Second Edition*, edited by John M. Reilly. New York: St. Martin's Press, 1985, cloth, p. 757-758.

Bakerman, Jane S. "Ruth Rendell," in *10 Women of Mystery*, edited by Earl F. Bargainnier. Bowling Green, OH: Bowling Green State University Popular Press, 1981, cloth, p. 127-149.

Budd, Elaine. "Ruth Rendell: Terror Times Two," in *13 Mistresses of Murder*. New York: Frederick Ungar Publishing Co., 1986, cloth, p. 105-113.

Cooper-Clark, Diana. "Interview with Ruth Rendell," in *Designs of Darkness: Interviews with Detective Novelists*. Bowling Green, OH: Bowling Green State University Popular Press, 1983, cloth, p. 125-144.

Keating, H. R. F. "Ruth Rendell: *A Judgement in Stone*," in *Crime and Mystery: The 100 Best Bets*. New York: Carroll & Graf, 1987, cloth, p. 183-184.

A JULIAN SYMONS CHRONOLOGY

1912 Julian Gustave Symons born May 30th in London.

1929 Serves as a shorthand typist and secretary for an engineering company (through 1941).

1937 Founding Editor, *Twentieth Century Verse* (through 1939).

1941 Marries Kathleen Clark.

1944 Works as a advertising copywriter (through 1947).

1945 Publishes first novel, *The Immaterial Murder Case* (U.S. edition, 1957).

1947 Publishes *A Man Called Jones*. Serves as a reviewer for the Manchester *Evening News* (through 1956).

1949 *Bland Beginnings*.

1950 *The Thirty-First of February* (U.S. edition, 1951).

1953 Co-founder of the Crime Writers Association. Publishes *The Broken Penny*.

1954 *The Narrowing Circle* (U.S. edition, 1955).

1956 *The Paper Chase* (published in the U.S. in 1957 as *Bogue's Fortune*).

1957 Receives a Crimes Writers Assocation Award. Publishes *The Colour of Murder* (U.S. edition, 1958).

1958 Reviewer for the *Sunday Times*, London. Publishes *The Gigantic Shadow* (reprinted in the U.S. in 1959 as *The Pipe Dream*). Serves as Chairman of the Crime Writers Association (through 1959).

1960 *The Progress of Crime* and *A Reasonable Doubt: Some Criminal Cases Re-Examined* (nonfiction).

1961 *Murder! Murder!* (collection). Receives an Edgar Award from Mystery Writers of America.

1962 *The Killing of Francis Lake* (published in U.S. as *The Plain Man*) and *The Detective Story in Britain* (nonfiction).

1964 *The End of Solomon Grundy.*

1965 *The Belting Inheritance* and *Francis Quarles Investigates* (collection).

1966 *Crime and Detection: An Illustrated History from 1840* (published in the U.S. as *A Pictorial History of Crime*). Receives a Crime Writers Association Award.

1967 *The Man Who Killed Himself.*

1968 *The Man Whose Dreams Came True* (U.S. edition, 1969).

1970 *The Man Who Lost His Wife* (U.S. edition, 1971).

1972 *The Players and the Game* and *Bloody Murder* (published in the U.S. as *Mortal Consequences*).

1973 Receives an Edgar Award. Publishes *The Plot Against Roger Rider.*

1974 Serves as Editor for the Penguin Mystery Series (through 1979).

1975 Named Fellow of the Royal Society of Literature. Publishes *A Three-Pipe Problem.* Visiting Professor, Amherst College, Massachusetts (through 1976).

1976 President of The Detection Club (through 1985).

1977 Receives Swedish Academy of Detection Grand Master Diploma.

1978 Publishes *The Blackheath Poisonings* and *The Tell-Tale Heart: The Life and Works of Edgar Allan Poe*.

1979 *Conan Doyle: Portrait of an Artist*.

1980 *Sweet Adelaide: The Modern Crime Story*.

1981 *Tom Adams' Agatha Christie Cover Story* (reprinted in the U.S. in 1982 as *Agatha Christie: The Art of Her Crimes*).

1982 Receives a Grand Master Award. Publishes *The Detling Murders* (U.S. edition, 1983, as *The Detling Secret*).

1983 *The Name of Annabel Lee* and *Crime and Detection Quiz*.

1985 *The Criminal Comedy of the Contented Couple* (U.S. edition, 1986, as *A Criminal Comedy*) and *Dashiell Hammett*.

1987 *Makers of the New: The Revolution in Literature, 1912-1939*.

1988 *The Kentish Manor Murders*.

1989 Edits *The Essential Wyndham Lewis* (a collection of stories).

1990 *Death's Darkest Face*.

Julian Symons

V.

AN INTERVIEW WITH JULIAN SYMONS

SALWAK: You are an amazingly prolific man—short stories, plays, detective novels, poetry, criticism and reviews, biographies, histories. Have you always been so bursting with things to say?

SYMONS: I don't think of myself as especially prolific, although other people say I am. It's true that I do a lot of different things. I enjoy writing crime stories, but shouldn't be satisfied to do that and nothing else. Hence criticism, biography, social history, military history. I suppose I have used the money got from writing crime stories to finance books inevitably less profitable which I wanted to write, but I've rarely been conscious of doing so at the time.

There was a period early in the sixties when I became much absorbed in Victorian military history, and produced two books about aspects of it, *Buller's Campaign* and *England's Pride*, each of which represented roughly a year's work. They sold reasonably enough as such books go, and got a lot of critical attention; but I knew before I began that I couldn't possibly afford to write them without producing a crime story or two in the same period. Hence, when I'm working, which means doing research as well as writing, on a subject likely to bring a small financial return, I usually do this in tandem with a crime story, or in the now fairly distant past with a play for TV. I wouldn't recommend this as a way of working, but it seems to suit me.

Reviews and longer critical pieces are another matter. I've written critical articles since my early twenties, and feel uneasy if a month passes without my having something reviewable on hand. When I spent a year at Amherst College, from 1975 to 1976, I rather missed reviewing, even though the *Sunday Times*, for which

I've written regularly since 1958, kept in touch and sent books across the Atlantic to me. I particularly enjoy writing long pieces in the *Times Literary Supplement* and the *New York Review of Books*.

SALWAK: Do you have any literary regrets?

SYMONS: I should have liked to write a novel that I could truly believe was a masterpiece in the crime genre, to have written a few poems that I could think of as permanently important. I wish I could think I had done such things. No mock modesty involved. No modesty, even: I probably think better of my best crime stories than all except a few of my readers do, but I also see their limitations, and I know myself the most minor of minor poets. I think the best of my biographies, those on Carlyle and Poe, and perhaps on my brother, A. J. A. Symons, are underrated, but still they aren't as good as they might have been if I'd spent double the time on them.

SALWAK: Might you have written fewer works more memorably, if you'd never published a crime story?

SYMONS: It's an interesting question, to me at least, but in the end a pointless one. Better to accept that what happened was inevitable, the natural product of a period and of a personality. This shouldn't be taken as an expression of dissatisfaction. I've enjoyed what I've done, with a few exceptions when I've published work that should have been rejected, for reasons purely financial. If I were marking my card, however, I should say: "Might have done better." Which may, of course, itself be taken as a mark of conceit.

SALWAK: In writing crime novels, what sparks your imagination?

SYMONS: Different things. In the case of *The Thirty-First of February*, the fact that I worked in advertising for more than three years, and was able to use it as a powerful background. In *The Progress of a Crime*, a real-life crime that I found absorbingly interesting, when half a dozen boys pulled another off a bus, and one of them stabbed him to death while doing so. The problems of the value of eyewitness evidence, the methods of police interrogation in such cases, are carried over into the book. I may start from an odd incident, an unsolved real-life puzzle: *The Blackheath Poisonings* had its origins in a case that occurred at Croydon, which I set back more than thirty years in time. Sometimes even from a title that seems so good that I begin to spin a story to suit it: *The Criminal Comedy of the Contented Couple*, a recent book, comes to mind.

It's important to note, though, that one *uses* reality, and doesn't reproduce it. Reality is almost always clumsy, inartistic, something to mold into the shape you need as a writer. *The Progress of a Crime* needed all sorts of touches and improvements and additions before the real-life crime could become what was for me a satisfying crime story.

SALWAK: Why did you use Inspector Bland as a series character?

SYMONS: Bland was an accident, an error, someone who should not have been born. In my first three crime stories I didn't know what I was doing, or wanted to do, in the genre. *The Thirty-First of February* is the first book I can contemplate with any pleasure.

SALWAK: What are the pros and cons of writing a mystery series?

SYMONS: I'll repeat what I've often said before. *Pro* is general coziness, the fact that readers find a character they know and have grown fond of, as comforting as carpet slippers. For the writer he is a ready-made character. There's no need to introduce him. The reader knows his face, his love life (if any), his methods.

Con is the fact that if you want to show characters involved in emotional conflict, this kind of detective is like grit in the machinery. He demands attention all the time, he has to be the pivot round which the story moves, and this tends to dictate the kind of book it's possible to write. If you don't want this kind of restriction, then you should avoid the series character. And that's what, after the unfortunate flirtation with Bland, I have done. I'm used to publishers telling me that this decision has been commercially foolish. I'm sure they are right, and I don't mind.

SALWAK: How much of a novel do you actually work out before writing a first draft?

SYMONS: I rarely plot a story closely in advance, finding that rather stultifying. On the other hand, some disasters have come from thinking I had a good idea, and starting to write without fully considering its implications and limits. In consequence I've gone sailing happily along for about 20,000 words, and then—then it's apparent that although I may have had a good idea, it wasn't one that would bear the weight of a full-length novel. The best way for me (and all such statements, I think, have no more than personal validity, there's no "best way" for everybody) is to have a rough idea of the story, and the way in which I'm going to develop and pace it, so that I know a particular crucial event will occur a third of the way through, another two-thirds of the way, and so on—but not to have a cut-and-dried plot. Usually I know the ending, but not just how it will be achieved. I like the ending to have an element of surprise.

SALWAK: You seem in your novels less bound by tight construction than, say, Catherine Aird or P. D. James. Would you care to comment?

SYMONS: Without making comparisons, I think it's probably true that most of my books are fairly loosely constructed. Or, to put it in a way more congenial to me, that I like the idea of some freewheeling taking place, a story shifting in tone and even in style during its course. The three *Man Who...* books seem to me to do this well and engagingly, so that they contain many small surprises for the reader: as in *The Man Who Killed Himself*, when Arthur Brownjohn invents a character and is then horrified to find this nonexistent figure apparently coming to life. These seem to me successful crime stories, and good novels as well.

SALWAK: You have long been a student of the crime novel, and in a series of articles and monographs have given careful thought to the potentialities of the crime story as serious literature. Is there a fine line between the crime novel and the "serious novel"?

SYMONS: The line is fine, certainly, and as I've suggested in *Bloody Murder* it's drawn in different places by each reader concerned with such things. For me "serious" means seriously intended, and that implies a writer putting into a story something of his own beliefs and attitudes, about society as a whole or some element in it. This isn't a recipe for two-faced moralities, although it may sound that way. What made Evelyn Waugh a fine novelist? His skill in orchestrating stories and writing dialogue, yes, but also the basic seriousness in such an apparently casual story as *A Handful of Dust*, or the Crouchback trilogy. Nor does the writer necessarily set out to "express" anything. *Red Harvest* and *The Glass Key* offer powerful criticism of American politics and the shape of American society, but Dashiell Hammett didn't set out with the purpose of writing "social criticism," he just put some of his own beliefs into the books. The dismal thing about the crime story as pure "entertainment" is that the books are mostly so slackly written and lacking in individuality that they can entertain only on the lowest level. There are exceptions, of course, like the work of Emma Lathen and Michael Gilbert.

SALWAK: Does the crime novel have a social responsibility? What about one's individual responsibility as a writer?

SYMONS: The "detective novel" itself has no social responsibility, but writers have them, just like other people. What are they?—whatever we think they are. If you asking whether the crime writer has a "responsibility" to see that right triumphs, I shouldn't accept that for a moment, since views differ markedly about what is right and wrong. I think that most of Mickey Spillane's writing is detestable in its social implications, but I don't doubt that Spillane thinks that the murderous thugs he calls heroes are pillars of his society.

SALWAK: Would you agree that your world view is a bit cynical?

SYMONS: I've tried in my crime stories, and in the biographies too, for that matter, to put down the relationships between people as I see them operating. Often they are unsatisfactory, especially within families. I don't believe it is cynical to record these realities on paper.

SALWAK: In what ways have you been influenced by Wyndham Lewis?

SYMONS: Lewis seemed, and still seems, to me a man with a unique insight into the nature of the society in which I spent my formative years, the late twenties and early thirties. He was also in my view a great visual artist and writer of fiction up to around 1940. His later decline was steep—although *Self-Condemned*, which came out in the fifties, is a fine novel. I learned from Lewis, and to a much lesser degree from George Orwell, to distrust orthodoxies, to be suspicious of authority while acknowledging that it must always exist, to regard intellect as supreme, while recognizing that intellectuals often talk bigger, more fantastic nonsense than anybody else. All of these views have indirectly influenced my crime stories and biographies, and I suppose make up the attitude towards the world you have suggested as "a bit cynical."

SALWAK: Do you see yourself as writing within the English tradition of detective fiction?

SYMONS: Yes, I think I write more or less in an English tradition of crime fiction, always (for example) offering a puzzle to be solved. But not in a Golden Age tradition or anything like it. My books, along with many others nowadays, flout Golden Age beliefs about the triumph of morality and the law.

SALWAK: Looking at the type of novels you write, is there behind them an assumption that justice will be done by the law?

SYMONS: On the contrary, what I've been concerned to point out more than once or twice (in *The Progress of a Crime*, for instance) is the clumsiness, uncertainty, and occasional downright stupidity of justice administered by law. My view would be that "justice" as an abstract entity doesn't exist, and that legal justice often operates idiotically. At the same time I'd accept that some system of justice has to exist. It should be operated as nearly as possible impersonally, but we should not make the mistake of believing that it *is* impersonal. A judicial system must always be on the side of the *status quo*, whether democratic or totalitarian, against whatever forces are trying to upset it.

SALWAK: P. D. James has said, when asked how she researches a novel, that "It's not the things I don't know that get me into trouble, but the things that I *thought* I do know."

SYMONS: Indeed, indeed, very cogent. One does research, but of course only in areas where it seems to be needed. An example of an error in my own work can be seen in *The Blackheath Poisonings*, a book set in the 1890s. I have a character paying for something with a pound note. As more than one reader has kindly pointed out, pound notes didn't come into existence until 1914. Before then, the golden sovereign was sovereign.

SALWAK: How do you account for the continued growth of the crime genre in both Britain and America, and the continued pre-eminence of women writers.

SYMONS: The answer is in part commercial: books go on being written and published in great profusion because there is a steady market for them. A more interesting aspect of the question is why the Anglo-American crime story is so highly valued in countries where English is *not* the first language. It is partly because English is the nearest thing to a universal language, read, for example, by most literate Scandinavians. How many publishers' offices contain editors who can read Swedish, Danish, or Dutch stories in the original? Very few. So such works have to be sent to outside editors, an expensive proposition at best. So they aren't generally sent out at all, with a few exceptions (Sjöwall and Wahlöö, for example). I've been prophesying the emergence of national crime stories in various countries for years now, and there are interesting developments in Sweden, Canada, and perhaps Japan, but progress has been slower than I expected. Anglo-American supremacy is not seriously threatened.

SALWAK: For decades, critics have said that the traditional mystery is dead. As long ago as 1888 a review of the latest Sherlock Holmes story predicted the death of the genre. Yet it has continued to flourish. Why?

SYMONS: The crime story as a literary form springs from bourgeois society and is part of it. This is true of spy stories like those of Le Carré and Deighton, old-fashioned neo-Golden Age stories like Catherine Aird's, blackish novels like Ruth Rendell's, Patricia Highsmith's, and some of mine, and many varieties of American stories, both tough and tender. While bourgeois society exists, with its various appetites that need feeding, the crime story will flourish.

It does not flourish under a dictatorship, whether Russian, German, Spanish, or South American. It is in part a bourgeois pipe dream, in part a useful surrogate for violence.

SALWAK: You have said elsewhere that a crime writer must first of all be an entertainer. What else is he?

SYMONS: Crime fiction (including spy and adventure stories) must first of all be readable to sell, much more so in general than "straight" novels. Why? Primarily because of that strong central pole of narrative already mentioned. Of course there are particular things readers like in each kind of story—the excitement of the double, triple, and quadruple cross in the spy story, the excitement of action in the adventure thriller (of which Dick Francis is a fine exponent), the increasing tension and unease in a good psychological story, the coziness of modern versions of Golden Age fiction—but the thing joining these all these forms of sensational fiction is the continuous narrative, driven energetically along, which is almost deliberately avoided by many "straight" novelists. There are lots of exceptions to such a sweeping statement, but as a generalization I think it's true that this is the prime reason for the wide readership of crime fiction. It's worth remarking, however, that this readership has its limits. In all except a very few cases, crime novelists are read through library borrowings or in paperback. The great majority still have fairly small hardback sales.

SELECTED SECONDARY BIBLIOGRAPHY

Carter, Steven R. "Julian Symons and Civilization's Discontents," in *The Armchair Detective* (January, 1979): .

Cooper-Clark, Diane. "Interview with Julian Symons," in *Designs of Darkness: Interviews with Detective Novelists*. Bowling Green, OH: Bowling Green State University Popular Press, 1983, cloth, p. 173-186.

Grimes, Larry E. "Julian Symons," in *Thirteen English Gentlemen of Mystery*, edited by Earl F. Bargainnier. Bowling Green, OH: Bowling Green State University Popular Press, 1985, cloth, p. . .

Keating, H. R. F. "Julian Symons: *The Man Who Killed Himself*" and "*The Players and the Game*," in *Crime and Mystery: The 100 Best Bets*. New York: Carroll & Graf, 1987, cloth, p. 133-134, and 159-160.

Woodcock, George. "Symons, Julian (Gustave)," in *Twentieth-Century Crime and Mystery Writers, Second Edition*, edited by John M. Reilly. New York: St. Martin's Press, 1985, cloth, p. 834-836.

ABOUT DALE SALWAK

Dale Salwak is a Professor of English at Citrus College in Southern California. He was educated at Purdue University, and then at the University of Southern California under a National Defense Education Act competitive fellowship program. His publications include literary studies of John Wain and A. J. Cronin, and reference guides to the works of Kingsley Amis, John Braine, A. J. Cronin, Barbara Pym, Carl Sandburg, and John Wain. He has also edited four collections: *Literary Voices: Interviews with Britain's "Angry Young Men"* (Borgo Press), *The Life and Work of Barbara Pym*, *Philip Larkin: The Man and His Work*, and *Kingsley Amis: In Life and Letters*. His detailed study of *Kingsley Amis: Modern Novelist*, for which he was awarded a National Endowment for the Humanities grant in 1985, will be published in 1992. In 1987 Purdue University awarded him its Distinguished Alumnus Award. Dr. Salwak was recently named Editor of The Milford Series: Popular Writers of Today, a lengthy series of literary critiques published by The Borgo Press.

Adams, Tom, 97
Addison, Joseph, 5
Agatha Christie, 60, 97
Agatha Christie Cover Story, 97
Aird, Catherine, 5-34, 102, 105
Aldrich, Pearl G., 34
Allingham, Margery, 17, 40, 70
Auden, Wystan Hugh, 40, 52
Austen, Jane, 6, 18, 56
Austin, Gerald, 87, 91
Bacon, Francis, 5
Bakerman, Jane S., 94
Bargainnier, Earl F., 94, 106
Bats Fly Up for Inspector Ghote, 60
The Belting Inheritance, 96
Benstock, Bernard, 57
The Best Man to Die, 81
The Black Tower, 36, 49
The Blackheath Poisonings, 97, 100-101, 105
Bland Beginnings, 95
Blood on the Mind, 60
Bloody Murder, 71, 96, 102
The Body in the Billiard Room, 61
The Body Politic, 12, 28-29
Bogue's Fortune, 95
Boucher, Anthony, 11
Brave New World, 6
The Bridesmaid, 83
The Broken Penny, 95
Brooke, Rupert, 40
Browning, Robert, 79
Buchan, John, 17
Budd, Elaine, 57, 94
Buller's Campaign, 99
Carlyle, Thomas, 100
Carmichael, Harry, 18
Carr, John Dickson, 17
Carter, Steven R., 106
"Catherine Aird's Comfortable Corpus," 34
Chandler, Raymond, 40
The Chinese Orange Mystery, 17
Chislet and Westbere, 12
Christie, Agatha, 41, 56, 60, 63, 97
Christie, John Reginald Halliday, 89
Clark, Kathleen, 95
"Clinical World of P. D. James," 57
Collected Short Stories, 82
The Colour of Murder, 95
The Complete Steel, 11, 23
Conan Doyle, Portrait of an Artist, 97
Cooper-Clark, Diana, 57, 94, 106
The Copper Peacock, 83
Corneille, Pierre, 6
Cover Her Face, 35, 51-52
Crime and Detection Quiz, 97
Crime and Detection, 96
Crime and Mystery, 61, 79, 94, 107
Crime and Punishment, 49
Crime Writers, 61
Crime Writers Association, 12, 35, 60-61, 82, 95-96
The Criminal Comedy of the Contented Couple, 97, 101
Critchley, Thomas A., 35
Crofts, Freeman Wills, 9
Crouchback Trilogy, 103
A Dark-Adapted Eye, 82
Dashiell Hammett, 97
A Dead Liberty, 12, 29
Dead on Time, 61
Death and the Visiting Firemen, 59, 64
Death Notes, 82, 89-91
Death of a Fat God, 59
Death of an Expert Witness, 36, 55
Death's Darkest Face, 97
Deighton, Len, 76, 105
A Demon in My View, 82, 90
Designs of Darkness, 57, 94, 106

The Detection Club, 97
The Detective Story, 96
The Detling Murders, 97
The Detling Secret, 97
Devices and Desires, 36
Dobkin, Harry, 27
The Dog It Was That Died, 59
Dostoevski, Fëdor Mikhailovich, 49
Doyle, Arthur Conan, 17, 40, 75, 90
Edgar Award, 35-36, 60-61, 82, 96
"Emma," 6
The End of Solomon Grady, 96
England's Pride, 99
Essays on Detective Fiction, 57
Essential Wyndham Lewis, 97
The Face of Trespass, 82
The Fallen Curtain, 82
A Fatal Inversion, 82
"Fen Hall," 92
Filmi, Filmi, Inspector Ghote, 60
Fordwich: The Lost Port, 12
Francis Quarles Investigates, 96
Francis, Dick, 106
From Noon with Death, 81, 87
Gallowglass, 83
Gaudy Night, 41
Gidez, Richard B., 57
The Gigantic Shadow, 96
Gilbert, Michael, 103
The Glass Key, 103
Go West, Inspector Ghote, 61, 73-74
Going Wrong, 83
Gold Dagger, 60-61, 69, 82
The Governess, 78
Gray, Thomas, 8
Great Crimes, 61
Greene, Graham, 56, 71
Grimes, Larry E., 106
A Guilty Thing Surprised, 81
Hammett, Dashiell, 40, 97, 103

A Handful of Dust, 103
Harkness, Bruce, 57
Heartstones, 82
Heilbrun, Carolyn G., 57
Henrietta Who?, 11, 26
Herbert, Rosemary, 34
Highsmith, Patricia, 105
Hill, Reginald, 79
His Burial Too, 11, 27
The House of Stairs, 82
How to Sell Bestselling Fiction, 34
Hume, William Douglas, 79
"I Am a Camera," 21
The Iciest Sin, 61
The Immaterial Murder Case, 95
In Sickness and in Health, 81
Innes, Michael, 63
Innocent Blood, 36, 40, 43, 45-47, 49, 55
Inspector Ghote Breaks an Egg, 60
Inspector Ghote Caught in Meshes, 60
Inspector Ghote Draws a Line, 61
Inspector Ghote Goes by Train, 60
Inspector Ghote, His Life and Crimes, 61
Inspector Ghote Hunts the Peacock, 60
Inspector Ghote Plays a Joker, 60
Inspector Ghote Trusts the Heart, 72
Inspector Ghote's Good Crusade, 60
Into the Valley of Death, 78
Is Skin-Deep, Is Fatal, 60, 69-70
"Is There Still an English Cozy Mystery?," 34
Isherwood, Christopher, 21
Jacobson, Jeanne M., 34
James, Henry, 79
James, Montague Rhodes, 88
James, P. D., 6-7, 9, 35-57, 101, 104
Joyner, Nancy C., 57
A Judgement in Stone, 82

"Julian Symons and Civilization's Discontents," 106
Keating, H. R. F., 6-7, 58-80, 94, 107
Keating, Maurice, 60
The Kentish Manor Murders, 97
The Killing Doll, 82, 91
The Killing of Francis Lake, 96
Koontz, Dean R., 34
The Lake of Darkness, 81-82, 91
Last Respects, 12
A Late Phoenix, 11, 26-27, 31
Lathen, Emma, 18, 103
Le Carré, John, 105
Lewis, J. D., 25-26
Lewis, (Percy) Wyndham, 103-104
Live Flesh, 82
The Lucky Alphonse, 61, 74-75
MacInnes, Helen, 21
Make Death Love Me, 82, 91
Makers of the New, 97
A Man Called Jones, 95
The Man of Gold, 78
The Man Who Killed Himself, 96, 102
The Man Who Lost His Wife, 96
Man Whose Dreams Came True, 96
Master of the Moor, 82
The Maul and the Pear Tree, 35
McNeile, Cyril (pseud. Sapper), 17
The Meaning of Treason, 26
Means of Evil and Other Stories, 82
A Mind to Murder, 35, 49, 52
Mitchell, Gladys, 63
Mitchell, Sheila Mary, 59
"Moment of Power," 35
Mortal Consequences, 96
A Most Contagious Game, 11, 23-25
Mrs. Craggs: Crimes Cleaned Up, 61
Murder Being Once Done, 81
Murder Must Appetize, 60, 70
The Murder of the Maharajah, The, 61

Murder! Murder!, 96
Mystery Writers of America, 35, 60-61, 82, 96
The Name of Annabel Lee, 97
The Narrowing Circle, 95
The New Girl Friend, 82
A New Lease of Death, 81
The Nine Tailors, 9
Nineteen Eighty-Four, 6
No More Dying Then, 81, 91
"Ode on the Death of a Favourite Cat," 8
"On Being a Writer of Detective Fiction," 5-11
One Across, Two Down, 81, 91
"The Orchard Walls," 92
Orwell, George, 104
"P. D. James," 57
The Paper Chase, 95
Parting Breath, 12, 22
Passing Strange, 12
Payment Deferred, 91
The Perfect Murder, 60, 70
A Pictorial History of Crime, 96
The Pipe Dream, 96
The Plain Man, 96
The Players and the Game, 96
The Plot Against Roger Rider, 96
Poe, Edgar Allan, 97, 100
Progress of a Crime, 96, 100-101, 104
Punshon, E. R., 63
Put on by Cunning, 82
Queen Elizabeth II, 36
Queen, Ellery, 17
A Reasonable Doubt, 96
Red Harvest, 103
Reilly, John M., 34, 57, 79, 94, 107
The Religious Body, 11, 22-25
A Remarkable Case of Burglary, 60
Rendell, Donald, 81

Rendell, Ruth, 6-8, 81-94, 105
A Rush on the Ultimate, 59, 65, 67-68, 71
Ruth Rendell's Suffolk, 83
Sayers, Dorothy L., 9, 17, 40-41, 56, 63, 69
"The Scales of Justice," 12
The Secret House of Death, 81, 91-92
Self-Condemned, 104
Shake Hands Forever, 82
The Sheriff of Bombay, 61, 75-76
Sherlock Holmes, 61
Shroud for a Nightingale, 35, 47, 49-50, 53-55
Siebenheller, Norma, 57
Sins of the Fathers, 81
The Six Preachers of Canterbury Cathedral, 12
Sjöwall, Maj, 105
The Skull Beneath the Skin, 36, 53
A Sleeping Life, 82, 90
Slight Mourning, 12, 28
Snow, Charles Percy, 52
Some Die Eloquent, 12, 27
Some Lie and Some Die, 81, 91
A Sort of Life, 71
Speaker of Mandarin, 82, 92
"The Speckled Band," 17
Spillane, Mickey, 103
Staley, Thomas F., 57
The Stately Home Murder, 11
Steele, Richard, 5
The Story of Sturry, 11
Sturry: The Changing Scene, 11
Sweet Adelaide, 97
Symons, A. J. A., 100
Symons, Julian, 6, 8, 71, 95-108
Talking to Strange Men, 82
A Taste for Death, 36
The Tell-Tale Heart, 97

10 Women of Mystery, 57, 94
Tey, Josephine, 17-18
13 English Gentlemen of Mystery, 106
13 Mistresses of Murder, 57, 94
Thirty-First of February, 95, 100-101
A Three-Pipe Problem, 96
To Fear a Painted Doll, 81
The Tree of Hands, 82, 92
Tudor England, 5
"The Turn of the Screw," 79
Twentieth Century Verse, 95
Under a Monsoon Cloud, 61, 77
Undermining the Central Line, 83
The Underside, 60
Understanding Pierre Teilhard de Chardin, 60
Unguarded Hours, 83
An Unkindness of Ravens, 82
Unnatural Causes, 35, 53-54
An Unsuitable Job for a Woman, 36, 43, 54
Vanity Dies Hard, 81, 88, 90-91
The Veiled One, 82
Vine, Barbara—see: Ruth Rendell
Wahlöö, Per, 105
A Warning to the Curious, 82
Waugh, Evelyn, 56, 102
Wentworth, Patricia, 18
West, Rebecca, 26
White, Ernest C. B., 35
Whodunit, 61, 73
With Mallet Aforethought, 65
Wodehouse, Pelham Grenville, 44
A Wolf to the Slaughter, 81, 91
Woodcock, George, 107
Writing Crime Fiction, 61
Yates, Dorothy, 17
Zen There Was Murder, 59, 64

www.ingramcontent.com/pod-product-compliance
Lightning Source LLC
LaVergne TN
LVHW041631070426
835507LV00008B/564